Old Deeside Ways

Best Wishes

[signature]

Dedicated to Elizabeth

Without limiting the rights under copyright reserved here, no part of this publication may be reproduced, stored in or introduced into a retrieval system, or transmitted, in any form, or by any means (electronic, mechanical, photocopying, recording, or otherwise), without the prior written permission of the author of this book.
© copyright

Lochnagar Publications 2015

© Ian Murray
ISBN 978-0-9537480-1-3
Enquiries to Alt na Craig, Braemar Road, Ballater, Aberdeenshire, Scotland, AB35 5RQ
e-mail ianlochnagar1@btinternet.com
Web Site www.lochnagar.net

Foreword

The ways through the hills and glens are many as are the old ways of life. The title of this book can be taken to mean both but mainly ways of life. There would not have been roads and paths through the hills and glens if there were not reasons behind people's movements. The more subtle connections are among folk, their families and their occupations. Although this is a Deeside book, it connects through the people and their folklore from our glens and mountains and also far beyond this area to other parts of the world.

Upper Deeside has many unique attributes and highly-varied landscape, the ways of life here, especially in the outlying areas, were similar to how things were done throughout other Highland glens of Scotland. When I began writing I came to know the folk and the landscape well and I could see that their knowledge was in imminent danger of disappearing. My concern in wanting to preserve some of the folklore has resulted in four books but also led me into place-name study with Adam Watson, adding a fifth book to the collection. I have tried not to repeat myself as more knowledge has been gained: this can be difficult because some information is covered in earlier books then more becomes available at a later time. Because of this, although this book stands alone, the reader may find it useful to refer to my earlier books. The chapters in this volume feature folk some of whom are long departed, again unique individuals but also reflective of a way of life at that particular time, and sometimes, because photographs exist of them from that period, the lives they lived and the knowledge of the area about which I feel passionately are relevant and contrasting with modern ways and technology of today. This is a contrast that only makes their lives more interesting to us now. There are still those among us as I write who worked with the horse and cart and remember the first motor cars and aeroplanes.

I am at the stage of realising, that after thousands of miles on foot, many excursions to rivers and streams and hundreds of taped interviews on the old ways, I have merely scratched the surface of a very special area. I probably did not need to go to such lengths but then my reward has been in meeting so many interesting people and experiencing this great area in a far more detailed way. Equally I can say with confidence that the same discoveries would never have been made and the books would have been more superficial and less authentic. The way in which the book is presented is through the best earliest sources I could find and I have left as much as possible of the anecdotes as they were told to me. To connect with a place at a deeper level might take perseverance and patience but ultimately the levels of awareness rise and a highly varied world of mountains, glens, rivers and especially folk emerges in glorious detail and infinite variety. The population to a large extent have left the glens. This book and its predecessors are a story of these folk and the places in which they lived and worked but not just in the past, also in the present day. Having taped many of our elders over some 26 years, I feel a sense of duty about publishing these findings. I also want to share some of my own experiences and discoveries. I am keeping in mind that someone may be reading these books decades from now. I hope you gain some enjoyment from this continuing adventure.

Yours Aye

Ian Murray

Ballater October 2015

Contents

Introduction			vi
Chapter	1	Ballater as it was born	1
Chapter	2	Glen Muick	7
Chapter	3	It's an ill wind for the Invercauld	19
Chapter	4	Mar Forest	25
Chapter	5	Ian Grant of Pinewood, Inverey	57
Chapter	6	Colour photographs of the area	83
Chapter	7	Howard Butterworth	91
Chapter	8	Paul Anderson	97
Chapter	9	Burn o' Vat	103
Chapter	10	The Battle of Culblean	111
Chapter	11	Sandy Davidson	129
Chapter	12	The last Ritchie o' the Torran	139
Chapter	13	The Last Wolf	147

Introduction

When I was a young boy growing up in Rothiemurchus, on the north side of the Cairngorms, one of the great events of the year was the Braemar Games. Every year a group of men from Rothiemurchus would walk through the Làirig Ghrù to the Games, as their forefathers had done for generations. They would always come back with tales of the people of the Braes of Mar with whom they had stayed or shared a dram during the course of the weekend. The way of life of these people, their concerns and their interests seemed to be so similar to ours, although we were separated from them by the highest mountain range in the British Isles.

Old Deeside Ways is very much about old Highland ways, as almost all the old natives of Mar featured in this book led a recognisably Highland way of life. In many parts of the Highlands, I have often heard the old people say that the Highlandman's right was to take "a tree from the forest, a salmon from the river and a deer from the hill" and occasionally added to this was "the right to make your own whisky." One of the people we meet, Ian Grant, was almost an embodiment of the old Highland ways: he spoke Gaelic, wore the kilt as his daily attire, was a Highland Games athlete, played the pipes, fiddle and accordion, lived an almost self-sufficient life on his croft in Inverey, and indulged in all four activities involved in the Highlandman's right.

The old natives of Mar we meet in this book come across as courageous, independent, highly principled individuals. Sandy Davidson is a notable example: though regarded by the authorities as a notorious poacher, he would never shoot out of season, nor on the Sabbath day, and though banned by the factor from Invercauld Estate, he risked his own life in order to save the same factor from death by drowning in the River Dee. Also, the gamekeepers of Mar in 1914, although dependent on the Royal Family for their livelihoods and their homes, were equally courageous sending a letter to the Princess Royal, signed by them all, requesting a pay rise, behaving almost like a gamekeepers' trade union.

The history of the fauna of the Braes of Mar is also featured. Although the last wolf in the British Isles is generally regarded as having been killed near Moy in Inverness-shire in 1743, we hear the tale of the killing of the last wolf in Glen Gairn, which locals assert post-dated the Inverness-shire event. This chapter is greatly enhanced by the inclusion of the music for two new compositions commemorating the event by well-known Tarland fiddler, Paul Anderson.

Since 2014 is the centenary year of the outbreak of World War I, it is interesting to hear of how the war one night physically reached the Cairngorms. On the night of the 2nd of May 1916, German Zeppelin L20, loaded with bombs, flew over Braemar and dropped a flare not far from the keeper's house at Luibeg. Fortunately this was done only in order to determine whether it was over land or sea.

This book is lavishly illustrated with photographs. There are some beautiful colour photographs from the present day and many monochrome photographs of the Braes of Mar in former times. The character and individualism of the old keepers and stalkers come across clearly in the older photographs. Particularly interesting are the photographs of the mountain rescue team, where we see how such teams in the Cairngorms were generally equipped until the 1950s: with brogues, plus-fours, gabardine coats and flat caps!

As well as oral history, a number of other subjects are covered in this book. The Battle of Culblean, which was an important battle during the Scottish Wars of Independence and took place at Culblean near Dinnet on St Andrew's Day 1335, is one of the interesting subjects included. The story of the ship Invercauld is a sorry saga: built in Aberdeen from Ballochbuie fir, it foundered off the coast of New Zealand in 1864, leaving its crew marooned on an uninhabited island for a year. There is also an interesting chapter on Howard Butterworth, an adopted son of Deeside and outstanding artist, whose paintings capture, not only the scenery, but the atmosphere of the district so perfectly.

Ian, through his series of books, has done so much to document the way of life, the culture and history of the people of the Braes of Mar. Indeed, thanks to him, their culture and way of life are probably the best documented of any community in the Cairngorms. If he had not undertaken the task of interviewing the old people of Mar in such a timely fashion and skilled manner, much of the history and the culture of the Cairngorms would now be lost and we would know so much less about the ways of life of our ancestors, about old Deeside ways and old Highland ways.

Dr Seumas Grant, 8 November 2014

Chapter 1   ***Ballater as it was born***   1

Ballater as the main settlement on Upper Deeside did not exist until the late 1700s. Where the town stands today was flat moorland used mainly by drovers passing through with herds of black cattle and sheep. The old picture painted before photography was around gives a great impression of what it was like then. Even in those days it was a tourist area with folk coming to drink from the mineral wells after Isabella Michie had cured herself by bathing in the bog at Pannanich and had been drinking the mineral water.

Ballater in 1797 showing from left Pannanich Lodge, the Bridge of Ballater and Bridge of Muick behind, Craigendarroch and Ballater or Monaltrie House right

The artist must have set up his easel at the head of the Tullich Brae, still a grand view point today. To the left of the picture is a substantial building right down next to the River Dee. This is clearly Pannanich Lodge, little of which remains today. The place was more or less forgotten but a stance of trees, a few stones and part of a bed remain.

The Lodge salmon fishing pool retains the name and often fishermen enquire why it has such a name. This is the reason: the lodge is not to be confused with Pannanich wells, still a fine building located farther to the East. The Statistical Account of Scotland 1791-1799 was written at the time of the painting and parts of it describe the few buildings that existed at that time.

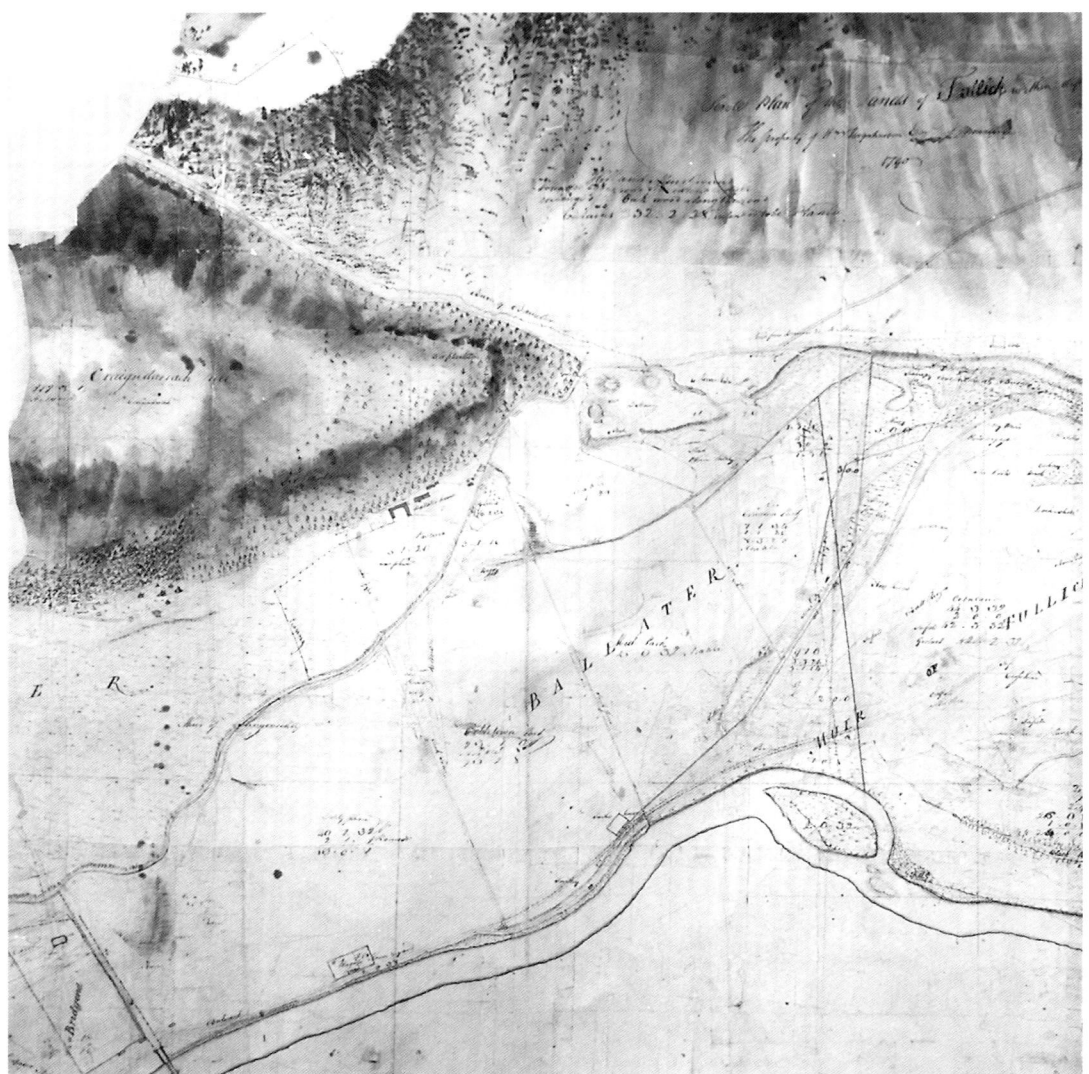

Ballater with its proposed bridge 1790 showing Ballater House at the foot of Craigendarroch

The wells being the property of the gentleman, already mentioned (Mr Farquharson) he cleared out the springs, which are three, and covered them; and erected not only feveral houses upon the fpot for the accommodation of the water drinkers, as a public and private bath, an octagon for the better sort to retire to, and several houses for sheltering the poor; but alfo built a large and commodious houfe called Pannanich Lodge, pleasantly situated upon the banks of the

BALLATER AS IT WAS BORN

Dee, about a mile W. of the wells containing a large public room, and a number of private ones, with accommodation for fervants and horfes, which, with a tolerable farm, and the houses at the wells, is let to a landlady at 50l. yearly who has the good fortune to give universal satisfaction to all vifit her.

Behind Pannanich Lodge in the picture is one of the Ballater bridges: the first was built in 1783 and lasted only a few years, being swept away by floods in 1789. The bridge shown in the painting must therefore, you would think, be the second stone Telford bridge. However our artist's date is 1797 and the second bridge was not built until 1809, lasting only until the Muckle Spate of 1829. The artist has shown behind the main bridge the bridge of Muick, but not the current bridge of Muick, which wasn't built until 1878.

Acrofs the Muick, and near the church, there is a very ufeful and fubstantial ftone bridge of one arch, built about 50 years ago by fubscription, and about half a mile below the

Ballater well established 1856

church, a beautiful bridge of three large arches, and a fmall one at each end, called the Bridge of Ballatar, was lately built by fubscription, and other contributions, under the patronage of the late Francis Farquarfon, Efq. of Monaltrie; a gentleman who has left many lafting monuments of his public fpirit in this country. In this parish are the celebrated wells of Pannanich, on the N. fide of a hill of the fame name, about 2 miles E. of the church.

Another building, Braichlie, can just be made out in the distance in Glen Muick, too early for the current Braichlie and predating the large Glen Muick house. Craigendarroch is prominent with some artistic licence and directly below is the Baron Ban's Ballater House or Monaltrie House, which he built after returning finally from England, having been taken prisoner and held there after leading the Farquharsons on Culloden Moor.

Former site of Pannanich Lodge from the Lodge Pool with Ballater in the distance

As for the wells, they had this to say in 1794;

They were difcovered accidentally to be of ufe, about 35 years fince, by an old woman living in the neighbourhood, who had for many years been distressed with fcrofulous fores; and who, after being reduced almost to the laft ftage of weakness and decreptitude, took a fancy (for fhe had no expectations of a cure) to crawl upon her crutches every good day to the wells, which were then a bog remarkable only for the blueifh fcum on the surface of the water; here fhe bathed her fores, and laid rags dipped in the water upon them; and perfevering in this course for fome time, fhe was agreeably furprifed to see her fores heal up, and to find her ftrength return. this brought the wells into immediate repute.

The town had become much more established by 1856, as can be seen by the early photograph, though it took quite some years to get going. Traditionally, I was told as a boy, the Farquharson laird came down with his factor and cut a furrow where he wanted the first streets to be. Even today Ballater has a much more planned and thought-out look to it than some other places. I went to see Sandy Alexander, former Burgh Surveyor and 100 years old at the time of interview.

Faan I was eleven I would come up Eastfield wi the milk cairt ye ken, a horse shelt, afore I gaed tae school. I mind faan the tar began tae come in on the roads, I mind my mother wi the margarine tryin to get the tar aff of our feet. Sandy recalled the quarries working at Cambus o' May eventually finishing because some of the rock was porous.

Ballater as a Burgh had its own council, provost and court. Sandy worked for three provosts in his time. *The first twa were proper gentlemen and the third was a proper lady. Faan the Burgh was on the go ye kent aathing that was going on you were much closer to aathing. There was a cooncilor, every now and again if it was raining he was out with his umbrella and he walked roond the streets if he struck a branch then the next council meeting a letter gaed oot to trim the tree or we will do it for you and charge you. Queen's Road on the right hand side was built by Grant, (Gracy Grant's grandfather) he built the whole lot and occupied them. Findlay was the only one wi a different name and he was mairried to a Grant, every one before my time and for a lang time in my time of day was a Grant. The Barracks* (in Queen's Road) *were built for a hot country, there was a mistake at the War Office but no one would admit to it so they were built like that. There is a barracks in India with our design and we got their plans.*

The old barracks buildings are noticeably different with steeply pitched roofs.

John Taylor, a former guard on the railway and fishing ghillie, told of the first-ever plane to come to the district, landing at Eastfield Park (date unknown), he was delivering biscuits to Balmoral.
The second plane to land at Ballater was 1937 or 1938 and was carrying a reporter from the Manchester Guardian newspaper who was to report on the Balmoral scene. Mr L Gillies of the Riverside Garage had been asked to light a beacon beside the garage and take down a fence so the plane could land safely. The plane flew up the Dee Valley over the nearby rubbish dump and the pilot mistook the burning rubbish for the beacon. The pilot started to land but by the time he realised his mistake it was too late and he was forced to crash land. The plane was damaged but the pilot was unhurt. The policeman on duty at the site was Mr George Lumsden and the wreckage was guarded all night by Mr Max Bannerman. The tip of the broken propeller was removed as a souvenir by Mr John Taylor and is still in the hands of a Ballater resident.

Two old short streets in Ballater, Deebank Road and Viewfield Place, used to have the by-names Sklaichie Brae (meaning gossipy) and Mary Jean's Brae respectively. Mary Jean was the registrar for Births, Marriages and Deaths officiating at the foot of the brae a long time ago. Or, as I once heard of a similar establishment in Aberdeen hatch, match and dispatch. So the small anecdote goes that a lady came down to register her newborn and when Mary reappeared there were *two inquisitive wifies standing nearby*. One enquired, *Fit wis it Jean, a boy or a girl? She replied; Fit does it maitter fit it is as lang as it's hale and wisely!*

Chapter 2 **Glen Muick**

The public road ends at a car park several miles up the glen from Ballater. For some perhaps that is the end of the road, but not for walkers. In the days of the drovers this was a main route. Glen Muick certainly has its place in history, the old drove roads converged at the Spittal (a resting place for drovers) and then continued over the Capel Mounth towards Glen Clova, an old Deeside way across the hills.

No one knows the Glen Muick hills like John Robertson. His father and grandfather were also gamekeepers there before him. John encouraged us to fish up there when we were boys. *You're better up there fishing than hingin aboot the streets!* Sound advice and it was always much more of an adventure for us in any case. John's father could remember the last of the drovers who stayed at the old Spittal: today that building can just be made out next to the road. He said t*he very last drover was an afa lad to snore, michty, you could hear him fae ootside the hoose.*

Road to The Spittal, Glen Muick

Approaching the end of the public road to the right is a rectangular ruin, known to a few as Tetabootie meaning in Scots most likely to look about you. I have often been asked why: we don't know for sure. However think back to when it was in use, it is right by the road side and herds of black cattle and sheep would be taken right past it's front door. This therefore may be sound advice. Also of course it has such a grand location.

In the mid 1990s the gamekeepers were out at the hind shooting and noticed something unusual across Loch Muick from Glas Allt Shiel. It turned out to be the debris from a large avalanche. They stopped for a closer inspection and when spying across the loch they could see deer stuck in the snow and some still moving. They got the boat out and went across the loch. Several animals were released from the snow. They had to shoot some due to their injuries and then leave because of darkness. It wasn't until the snow finally disappeared that they could get back and again using the boat, they removed numerous deer carcasses, some of which were floating in the loch. They took them away down the glen and buried them. The avalanche was located opposite Glas Allt Shiel (a grand old lodge put up by Queen Victoria at the far end of Loch Muick) and a few hundred yards to the west. It swept down the Loch Braes and through the birch trees. Gary Coutts was there and Duncan Watt, both gamekeepers, Gary thought the number of deer killed in total was 52. During a chat with John one evening he mentioned a place on Glen Muick I had not heard of. It had become known as Slaughter Braes due to a similar incident back in his father's time. It looks as though a large herd of red deer triggered an avalanche which sent them hurtling down the slopes, killing several scores of them, hence the name Slaughter Braes.

John used to head from The Spittal across to Moulzie at the head of Glen Clova where Margaret lived in their courting days. The push bike was the best and quickest method then for John, the trip by road is a long drawn out drive of considerably more miles than the direct hill track between The Spittal in Glen Muick and Glen Clova.

John Robertson of The Spittal 2015

I have spent many enjoyable evenings with John and Margaret Robertson and the first time I went as someone interested in the past Margaret's mother was there sitting quietly in a chair facing towards the window although I did not realise she was in the room at the time. When John went out to answer the phone she had been enjoying the conversation and told me she had been many years in Glen Clova. It transpired later that she was 100 years of age. She told me about the bed and breakfast establishment she ran in an old manse across the hill. She could remember folk going off to the Boer War and all the songs they used to sing at that time. She also ran the Post Office and Jean, her oldest daughter, was the postie in the glen. Women working as posties were issued with skirts but Jean didn't want that and wrote to the Postmaster in Forfar asking for a pair of trousers for the winter.

Dear Sir
The skirt measurements were not forgotten. A skirt is no use on my job where I have miles to cycle, streams to cross, & walls to climb. Just send me a uniform jacket and I'll wear my own trousers.
Yours Faithfully
Jean G. Cameron

So they issued her with made-to-measure trousers and called them officially Camerons after Jean Cameron of Glen Clova and often nicknamed Jeans. This apparently started a fashion for thousands of women which became very popular just after the war, I was interested to discover

Reflections on Loch Muick

a short film was also made of Jean on her rounds in Clova called The coming of the Camerons.

There was a place, a former dwelling, across there called the Shot o Bontyre which Margaret recalled was buried

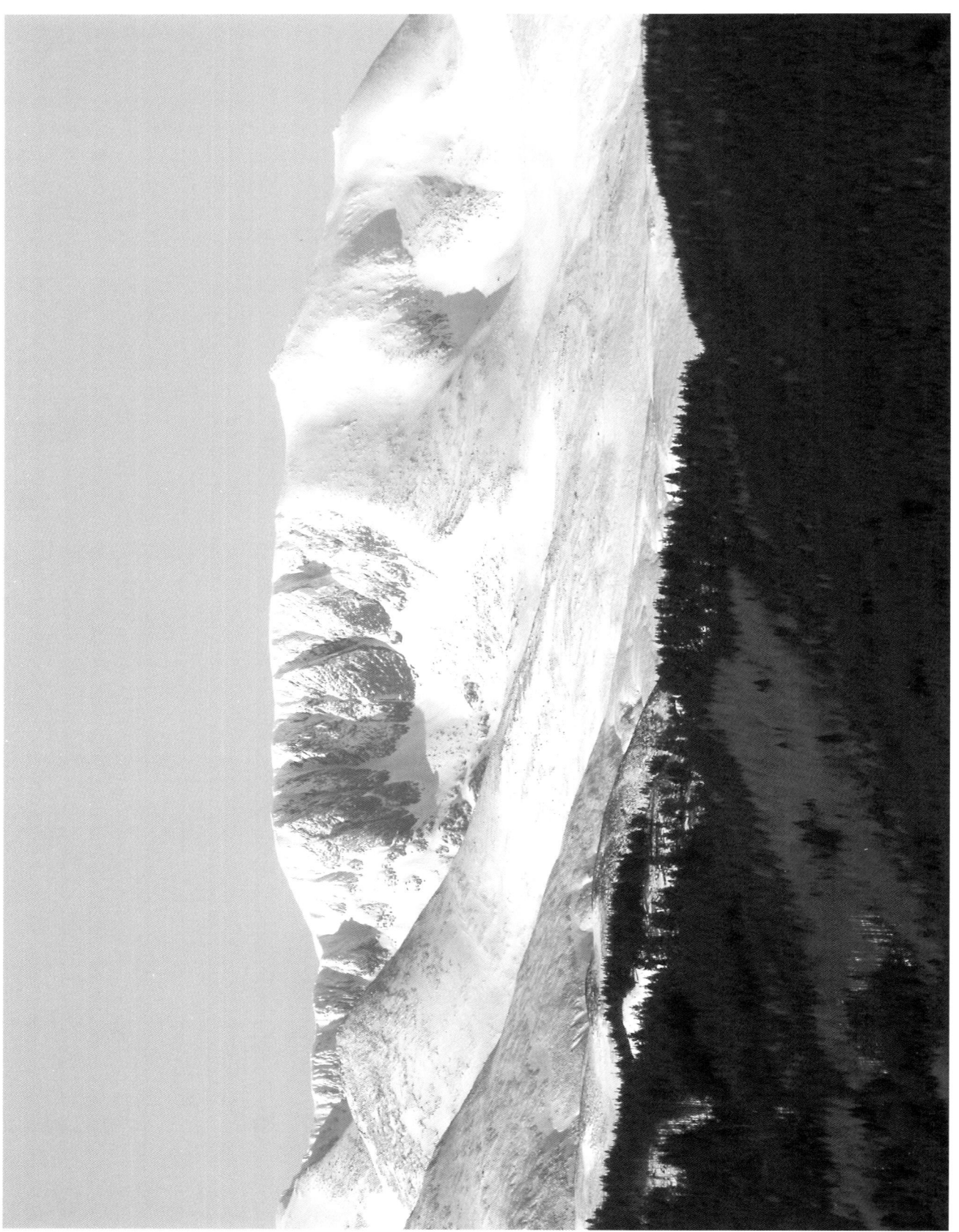

The main corrie of Lochnagar with Coire na Saobhaidhe to the right

long ago under a rock slide. The old folk used to say you could still hear the cock crow on a winny nicht. I have heard similar folklore at this side of the hill also. When Blair, the Queen's fiddler from Khantore, was discussed they said on a windy night if you listened carefully, you could still hear him play.

John told me of an old woman who lived across the hills in Glen Esk;

They say she could smell a rabbit in a dyke ye ken, she used to work her way along the dykeside then stop, put her arm into the dyke then out with a rabbit. Pull its neck and away hame wi it.

John had told me a story of one of those coincidences which can happen in life: as it involves Glen Muick and Lochnagar and far away places I thought well worth including here. Before there was an official organised rescue team mountain misadventures often involved the local bobbie and the gamekeeper on whose beat the incident had occurred. John had a spell as a spitfire pilot in the 1940s.

Matheson was the lassie's name that fell off Lochnagar that was some coincidence that I will tell ye. The aal man (John's father) was just about to leave when I come hame and he said I think we'll need to get help so I went doon tae the Crofts (farm at the foot of Glen Muick) Donald McHardy was there, of course. Aabody was awa at the war there was jist aald Willie McGregor at The Garbh Allt so we got him and Donald we got back up there first thing in the morning and searched and searched and searched and couldna find onything and aald Mac was as deaf as a post and by three o'clock we didna think she would be alive after a day and she'd been doon the face aald Mac said: that wisna a ptarmigan! So we said: what did you hear?

The strange thing was that no one else heard the noise.

I dinna ken what it wis but it wisna a ptarmigan. So we went in the direction he pointed and found this great boulder, started diggin and found her and got her oot and into the sleeping bag that we had at that time and we had three tins o self heating soup that we had so got them yokit and into the sleepin bag aside her. She was unconscious but still breathing and aathing, moaning a bittie.

They sledged her and carried her until they got her down and into the ambulance.

Time went on and John found himself posted abroad. *That was another thing you were not allowed to take money into India and it was twa months afore ye got paid then ye werena allowed to taak money oot: we got roond that.*

The Indian government although we were defending India charged for rent for erecting a tent and accommodation they had to pay for their digs didn't give us free medical attention either we had to pay for that so it was a brand new plane and I wis taakin it hame fae Santa Cruz in Bombay a brand new spitfire and I was putting it through its paces. The next thing I kent here was this covering strip far the wing joins part o the fuselage there were rivits started comin oot crikey I thought that shouldna be daein that then we started getting flutter this was the wing startin to rattle loose. So I cut the speed doon far as I could. They said bale oot but that's not so easy done faan there is something wrang like that I can tell you. I said no I'll land the damned thing. I came in withoot flaps I never let doon the flaps.

Aifter I had that tremendous crash I was in hospital and woke up, a bloody wing came aff and this ither ane comin up to meet it. They only put one bolt into the wing it wis my ain fault sort o thing that I took the wing aaf. I was just touching the ground and this wing started coming up so I put the seat doon and curled up inside the cockpit and put my hand ower my heid and that's the last I can mind of it. The control column hit me on the heid and fractured my skull. So I was lying in hospital then I come round and I didn't have a thing with me of course this nurse that was knocking aboot I saw she had been damaged aboot her face like and I said till her could she get me a pen and paper I said I will have to write to my folks to send out money to pay for this treatment so she did and I wrote to the aald folks. Aifter she was away with the letter she saw the address and she came back and said: were you one of the men that saved me when I fell off Lochnagar? That is why she had a damaged face when we found her doon the back o this steen how the hell she survived as long as she did she fell aboot 2 o'clock in the aifterneen she was right on the top of Lochnagar and stepped off and disappeared. When we found her doon the back of this steen she had obviously hit the steen head on.

GLEN MUICK

Left John Robbie, Jimmie Lowe, fishing ghillie, Jimmie Stewart.
Front kneeling Inspector Lachie, Angus Police, Alan Cameron, Donald Coutts Date unknown but pre Second World War

Old Byre at The Spittal of Glen Muick where the cow was kept

Her face was just a mass of blood the boy that was wi her he thought there was no point going that way either so he went the opposite way and landed back doon at The Spittal.

It was quite an amazing coincidence. When John returned to the Spittal after his active service, she often visited. John continued;

There is a glittering rock face ower to the right of Gelder Coire na Saobhaidhe we caad it.

The moss on the top o that glitterin rock it just slides aff ye ken there was a lad thought he would come doon that wye aff Lochnagar and into Gelder that wye but he got to this moss and it slid off and doon he come. The rest got doon and raised the alarm, we cairried him doon tae Allt na Giubhsaich. A lot o them used to come oot o the Black Spoot they would hit that damned big boulder ye ken. They came doon that same line like a chute. We were cairrying this lad oot and we were cairrying him the aal man (John's father) had a Bergen frame and he mounted a Tilley lamp on top.

That makes complete sense: anyone leaving the summit and heading down into the corrie can encounter smooth slippery rocks without much warning, of course made much more hazardous in winter.

At Glas Allt Shiel there was once a gamekeeper. Old McKenzie the keeper grew honeysuckle on a cairn away out the hill and grew tatties on the small island in front of Glas Allt Shiel where he was resident keeper, he put a weather vane on a large boulder away out the path towards the Dubh Loch. A small cairn on the cross path on Lochnagar still retains his name: it's called McKenzie's Cairn.

I asked John if he recalled any of the characters who used to come through that area.

There used tae be a lad came tae the Spittal, and used tae dae jobs and help with the hay he used to take the antlers which the keepers had collected and he could make them into a cube shape for selling. He also prospected for gold on his travels.

John's father would make food for him which he took outside: he wouldn't come inside. He just liked to work for his board and food then move on to the next place. He wasn't a tinker: he had a small army pension and just liked to roam.

Some way along lower Glen Muick is the farm of Aucholzie (field of woods) which once changed hands over a game of cards. The old lands of Aucholzie which extended from the source of the Muick on the south side to the Burn of Knockendow was owned by a Stewart but the lands were forfeited after his part in the 1745 Rising with Prince Charles Edward Stuart. According to the muster roll of the army, Alexander Stewart fought in the Monaltrie's and Balmoral regiment as a captain. He never saw Glen Muick again as he was killed at Culloden. He may well have gone home for a last time as many did for a short visit when the army crossed the Mounth on its way across to Culloden. The land was then taken over by the Earl of Aboyne, who held it for a few years before it was sold to Farquharson of

Invercauld. Tradition has it that Aboyne and Farquharson had met at Aucholzie, where a game of cards and a bowl of punch were suggested. It was proposed by Invercauld that, should he lose, he would pay the price asked by Aboyne, but should he win then Invercauld would have the estate free of any price. Aboyne was partaking too freely of the punch, it was said by old-time residents, and lost the game whereby Invercauld then as a gentleman offered to nullify the arrangement. Aboyne refused, stating that he wished to keep his promise and would have kept his promise even if the estate had extended to the *gates of Aboyne.*

Stewart the last laird of that name (according to old unpublished papers) was married to Barbara Farquharson, sister to Andrew Farquharson of Allargue, and aunt to a Charles Farquharson who was factor at Invercauld for some 45 years and known as The Muckle Factor. When he retired he was so highly thought of he was given Cluny Cottage, Braemar, with rights to fishing and shooting for his son and grandson. He died about 1817. There had been a heavy fall of snow and so it proved impossible to get him back to his family burial place in Strathdon. He was taken to Glen Muick as was the custom at the time, carried all the way with four carrying and changing over on the command of *ither fower* (Ceithir eile in Gaelic).

In 1860 some of the old residents still recalled seeing the body of the Muckle Factor being taken back to Glen Muick whereby the men involved experienced some difficulty due to the severe snowstorm. These old residents stated that they saw the funeral people *approaching by the Shoulder of the Craig of the Knocks, and a cloud rising from the men of their perspiration.*

John Robertson knew of a musical family in lower Glen Muick at The Knock. They were Littlejohns and there were seven or eight sons plus their father all of whom were stone masons.

They used tae walk fae there oot ower the Poolach and doon tae tae Etnach and build aa day then walk back again at night and they were also a band as well they would taak their instruments wi them ye ken, work aa day then oot ower the side o Mount Keen intae Tarf Side (another grand old way) *and then play at the dance there and walk back the*

Old Spittal house, Men from Dundee including Architect for Morven Lodge (craigendarroch) skied from Glen Clova

next morning. The foreman of the squad was away one day and left his bonnet. When he came back they had built it intae the waa and just left the snoot lookin oot.

He took the joke well and just took his trowel across the bonnet and knocked off the snout. He said: "If you lads can't build straight you will just have to go down the road", no doubt to great hilarity.

My mother was at Invermuick the coachman's place ye ken she used tae come doon there fae the Spittal faan she was first married in 1919 and winter, they didna stay at the Spittal aa winter at that time. There was a dog cart gaed up every morning ye see for the hinds and that she said this nicht aa the Littlejohns came trekin hame up fae Etnach ower the Brig o Muick coming hame and there was a dance in Ballater they were gaun tae be playin at. She said: "I dinna think there will be a dance the nicht." They were wadin to the knees in snaa, one behind the other heading to The Knock for their dinner. They said: "Oh aye there will be, we will come in past for you to take you to the dance:" and they did. Sure enough that was when they were building Etnach so that must have been about 1920.

There is more to write on this glen but time to move to another place on Deeside.

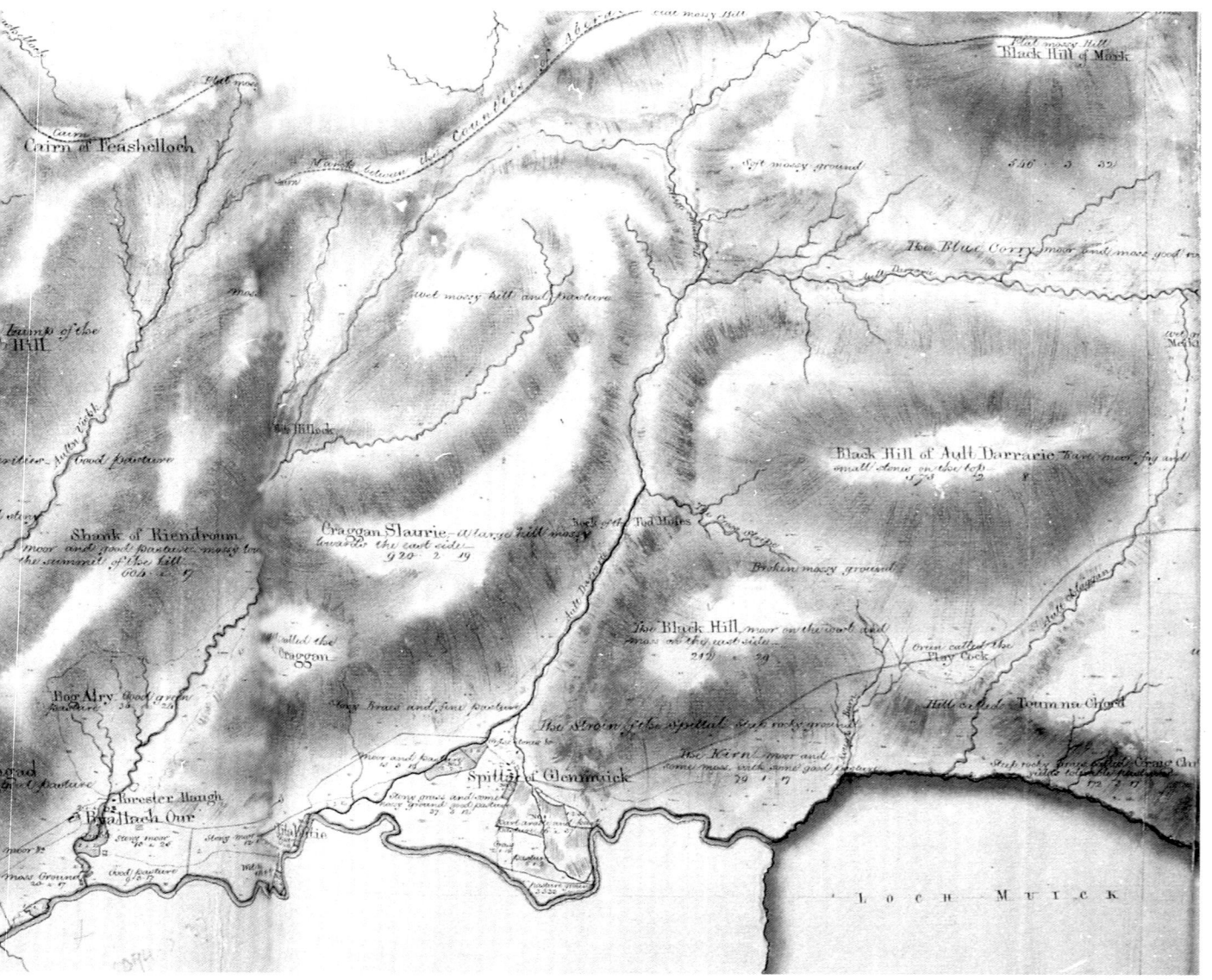

Spittal of Glen Muick 1808

Chapter 3   *An Ill Wind for The Invercauld*   19

She slipped out of Aberdeen harbour a brand new ship with the latest iron masts and rigging and twenty five men on board.

It's an ill wind, they say, that doesn't blow anyone any good, meaning of course, some good will come to someone unless it's a real ill wind. It certainly had a bearing on this story. The wind had been a factor when logs had been cut from Ballochbuie Forest, the trees having been flattened in a gale in the early 1860s. They were taken to Aberdeen, where they were skilfully fashioned into a ship, an innovation of her day. They named the ship Invercauld. She was an impressive 1100 tons.

Is the name the only link with Upper Deeside, I wondered, as if that were not enough? In fact, the Laird, Colonel Farquharson at the time, sent in venison and whisky to celebrate her launch and there was more. The crew which was made up of people from across the globe had a Middleton from Balmoral on board. Ballochbuie Forest used to be owned by Invercauld Estate before being sold on to become part of Balmoral Estate. It's an impressive forest holding one of the last remnants of the old Caledonian pine trees. I wonder if anyone passing under those old trees today makes a connection with the sea and the story of the Invercauld?

She set off on her maiden voyage on the 10th of January 1864, arriving at Melbourne on April 15th. She left then from Melbourne to Callao in Peru, for Guano on 2nd May. On the 10th of May of the same year, she was *in atoms.* The wind blew the trees down in the first place, the wind powered the ship across the world and the wind was a factor when it dashed the ship onto the rocks, smashing her to smithereens.

The trip was a disaster but the lucky ones got off the ship at Ballarat in order to pursue gold prospecting. The local connection more or less ended with the ship wreck, William Middleton, aged 19, being drowned *...The boys Middleton and Wilson, and four seaman were drowned.* The Press and Journal reported on 4th of November 1863...

Ballochbuie Forest looking towards Auld Brig o Dee and Beinn a' Bhuird to top right

There was a launch on Wednesday the 28th ultimo, from the building-yard of Mr. John Smith, Inches, one of those fine specimens of naval architecture, which has made Aberdeen so famous for its ship-building for some years past.

The vessel was named by Miss Smith, the builders' daughter, the "Invercauld" in honour of that highly esteemed gentleman, Colonel Farquharson of Invercauld, from whose forests part of the timber used in her construction was procured. She has a figurehead of exquisite workmanship, in full Highland costume, intended to represent the Chief of the Clan Farquharson, which is said to be a very striking likeness of the gallant Colonel....

She was captained by an Aberdonian, Mr George Dalgarno, aged 41

They went on to report... *she will be fitted with all the latest improvements in hull and rigging, and her saloon and cabins furnished and decorated in a most elegant style.*

The crew were from a wide area: among the list of places I cite this selection, Aberdeen, Russia, Gibraltar, Londonderry, Lerwick, Norway, Sweden, London, Dumfries.

She was sailing from Melbourne to Calla when she struck the Auckland Islands. The story might have ended there but a good proportion of the crew made it ashore and salvaged what they could to form a rough shelter from the timbers: that was the beginning of a long hard struggle. It seems they managed to salvage a little food, some pork and some biscuits.

Acknowledging permission of The National Library of New Zealand, the following gives a great insight and summary of the survival;

LETTER FROM THE CAPTAIN,

Captain Dalgarno, writing from Southampton to the owners, says : — I am at last offered another opportunity of addressing you again in this life, to let you know the sad and melancholy tidings of the ship Invercauld, which became a total wreck during the night of May 10th, 1864, on the island of Auckland, off New Zealand, during a heavy gale from the northward and thick weather. In about twenty minutes after striking, she was in atoms; so heavy was the sea running — and all rocks where the disaster happened The boys Middleton and Wilson, and four seamen were drowned; the remainder, nineteen of us. getting washed on shore through the wreck, all more or less hurt — the night being intensely dark and cold. We saved nothing but what we had on our persons ; and before being washed from the wreck, I hove off my sea boots, so as to enable me, if possible, to reach the shore. After getting ashore amongst the rocks, we called upon each other, and all crept as close together as we could. to keep ourselves warm. The spray from the sea reaching us made it one of the most dismal nights ever anyone suffered, and we were all glad when day broke on the following morning, when all who were able went toward the wreck to see what could be saved. All we found was about two pounds of biscuit and three pounds of pork - the only food we had to divide amongst nineteen; and after all taking about a mouthful each, we went and collected a few of the most suitable pieces from the wreck to make a sort of hut to cover us from the weather, where we made a fire, the steward having saved a box of matches. Dear Sir, I have seen and suffered more since the disaster happened than I can pen to you at this time ; but if God spares me to reach you

A rare picture of The Invercauld

I will then give you all particulars. We remained four days at the wreck, and having no more food, nor appearance of getting any more at the wreck, we proceeded to go on the top of the island to see if we could find food or any inhabitants. It was no easy matter to reach the top, it being about 2000 feet high, and almost perpendicular. "When we got there we found no inhabitants, and the only feed we found was wild roots that grew on the island, of which we ate, and fresh water. At night we made a covering of boughs, and, lighting a fire, crept as close together as possible. On the following morning we made towards a bay that was on the east side, which occupied some days, the scrub being so heavy to walk amongst. The cook and three seamen died during this time, and all of us were getting very weak for want of food and from cold. At length we reached the bay, where we found some limpets on the rocks, of which we ate heartily. We also caught two seals, and found them good food; and had we got plenty of them no doubt all would have lived. After living three months upon limpets they got done, and all we had again was the roots and water, seeing no more seals. By the end of August the only survivors were myself, mate, and Robert Holding, seaman; the carpenter, the boys Liddle and Lancefield, being among the last that died, all very much reduced. After we three had lingered for twelve months and ten days we were at last relieved by the Portuguese ship Julian, from Macao, for Callao, with Chinese passengers. She sprung a leak off here, and sent a boat on shore to see if they could get their ship repaired, when they found us the only inhabitants on the island. They proceeded on their passage to Callao, taking us three alone with them. We were treated very kindly, and on the 28th June reached Callao, where we were all treated kindly by the people there. On the same evening I sailed by the mail steamer for England, leaving the mate and the seaman in Callao. On the 6th July I sailed from Panama; on the 13th arrived at St Thomas, and sailed same day for Southampton by the steamship Shannon, meeting with the greatest kindness from all on board the several ships I sailed in.

Fish Market in Aberdeen 1887 note old-ship in background

24   OLD DEESIDE WAYS

Union Street Aberdeen 1887

Chapter 4 *Mar Forest and its Folk*

The folk of Mar Forest, like many Highland areas in Scotland, have had a long connection with the red deer and deer stalking as it's known today. It was the tradition in the area to have shooting lodges, sometimes known as shooting boxes, where the shooting tenants could stay, sometimes remotely out in the glens. Mar Lodge was a grand building, a version of which is still there today, located on an estate of the same name which reached to the highest tops. Corriemulzie was described on the OS map in the 1860s as Mar Lodge. On the same map Old Mar Lodge is marked where the current Mar Lodge is located. There is nothing left of Corriemulzie Mar Lodge apart from the dam and some outbuildings.

What was life like then for a well-to-do guest living in Mar Lodge in the 1800s?

My first day in Mar Forest by Horatio S.J.Ross Esq.

Driving the Deer on Ben MacDui, October, 1852.

The following is a brief account of my first day in Mar Forest when I was 17 years old and may be taken as a sample of the usual day's sport only that instead of a drive for deer, we sometimes merely stalked them.

Shooting party

I arrived at Mar Lodge after the season for shooting stags but was allowed by the Duke of Leeds to try and shoot any stag I might see with a good "head" never as yet having the good fortune to kill a stag.

7-AM Awake by hearing the piper playing the pipes in front of the house, my clothes and hot water bottle next make their appearance.

Alexander Grant, a former keeper on Mar Forest and father of Ian Grant

The Prince of Wales in the Highlands; A torchlight dance at Mar Lodge 1880

7-30 AM Jimmie Gow, the head forester comes to my room with a slate on which the Duke's orders for the day are written out & reads:- "Captain Ross and Mr. Horace Ross go to Glen Lui and have a drive.

Charles Fraser & Peter McHardy, Stalkers. James Fraser, Cattanach & Macintosh, Gillies. Bell and the white pony, ponies, Oscar and Bran staghounds, 'and' His Grace wishes you to be off in good time as the days are getting short now."

8-AM Breakfast in the large dining hall, surrounded by "Royals" & "Fourteen Pointers" excellent venison hash, Flask and sandwiches ready laid out on the side board. After breakfast, we mount the steeds and ride up to Machardy's house in Glen Lui, see herds of deer here and there on the hill sides.

A rare glimpse of life inside one of the old Mar Lodges

10-AM Leave ponies at Machardy's house, proceed to climb to the ridge of Cairn Gorm, 4000ft above the level of the sea, hear stags roaring in all directions.

11-30-AM Reach the top, magnificent view of snow clad hills, Ben Macdui with its corries and granite precipices, facing us on the other side of the glen only about a mile off. Cairn Toul rising its sharp blue peak above the corner of the former, Beny Glo and the Athol hills forming a beautiful broken line on the horizon. Herds of deer looking like small specks in the valleys and corries below us, packs of ptarmigan (now quite white in plumage) ever and anon fly past us and the air resounds with the roarings of stags some distance whilst an involuntary start is given as the gruff roar of a stag sounds quite close below us, a frosty blue sky and a balmy October sun.

MAR FOREST AND ITS FOLK

Shooting party heads out to Glen Lui

Now and then a stag would come trotting over the ridge of the hill having been driven away from the herd by some more powerful rival, we were not allowed to fire at deer then for fear of spoiling the 'drive'. At one part of the ridge there was a sort of dip in it forming a pass by which the deer were in the habit of crossing from the West to the East side of the hill. In a cairn of stones we settled ourselves in a position where we could fire at the deer coming through the pass. There were two other passes, at one of which, Fraser was placed with dogs and at the other, a gillie to keep the deer from passing that way. After waiting about an hour, (the men having had to make a long round) we hear the noise of stones rolling down the sides of the hills in the direction of Cairn Toul. 'They have begun now, we wanna have long to wait now' says MacHardy. Out come the spy glasses and the shoulder of Ben MacDhui opposite is eagerly watched. 'There they come' says my Father. 'Take the glass and have

The Duff Highlanders parade

a look' so spying in the direction pointed out to me, I saw a great drove of deer, stags and hinds mixed together coming hurrying over the shoulder of the hill.

'Look Captain' says Machardy, 'that stag near the hindmost part of the herd, has got a grand head, if the young gentleman could get a shot at him it would be a fine thing for him'. 'Yes, yes, I see him, says my father, 'He is a Royal, I'm sure and I rather think he has got four points on his left horn.' Now the herd reaches the burn directly below us, (only some 2000 feet beneath us) and a splashing and scrambling noise is heard as they cross. They are now lost to our view by the crest of the hill...ohr orh orh, the roar of the stag, is heard close under the bank, then the horns appear and a stag and four hinds come running past, a kind of advance guard. 'Fire at him' says my father, bang goes my rifle and away he goes lame of a hind leg, reload, shortly afterwards roars are heard from numerous husky throats and the great herd make

Golden Eagle chick sits on a rock eyrie, a dead grouse has been left by parent as food

32   OLD DEESIDE WAYS

Mar keepers

Ian Grant. Cornice formed by wind blown snow at the River Side

their appearance filling up the pass. At times some of them come within ten yards of where we are lying. 'If you want the young gentleman to get a shot of the big one, we must not fire till he comes says MacHardy, so we lie quite still whilst the deer file slowly past us with the breath streaming in the frosty air from their mouths and their tongues hanging far out. The last deer has passed the crest of the hill and still no signs of the big one, when a roar is heard and a fine ten pointed stag makes his appearance. 'You better shoot at him' says my father, 'the big one is not coming' so bang I go at him and away he goes hit but not mortally, my father then makes a beautiful running shot at a fat hind. (We are afterwards told by one of the gillies that the big fellow was following the ten pointer and turned back when I fired) we follow on after the wounded deer but see nothing of them, as it is getting dusk. I get one or two shots at deer on the way home but it is getting too dark to see the sights properly, next day we get one of the stags I wounded with the dogs. We ride home in the dark with a good appetite for an excellent dinner served up by a French cook, the best of venison, grouse entrées etc and no stint of champagne. After dinner, the Duke and the older ones smoke cigars and fight the day's battles over again, then tea with the Duchess in the Drawing Room, a game of Vingt at One (not for money) and off to bed. I remained at Mar Lodge for a fortnight and enjoyed myself very much. I shot one stag and six hinds during my stay. On September 22nd 1856, I left Dibidale, Ross-shire, for India, and returned to Dibidale in July 1863 a skinny invalid, when my real stalking in Ross-shire commenced.

The stalk of today is a vastly different business humanely done with high-powered rifle: the above gives insight to life at that time.

To Her Royal Highness,
　　The Princess Royal,
　　　　Mar Lodge
　　　　　　Braemar.

Mar Forest
　Braemar,

6/4/14.

May it please your Royal Highness.

We the undersigned Keepers in the employment of your Royal Highness desire most respectfully and humbly to approach you in the hope of obtaining an advance on our present wages which are £45 per annum. In view of the increased cost of living which has taken place in recent years, we feel that the purchasing power of our wages is now considerably diminished and an advance would accordingly be of great service and benefit to us.

For the consideration of your Royal Highness we would humbly and respectfully suggest that the wages might be advanced to £1 per week making the sum £52 a year in place of £45 as at present. Should our petition receive the favourable consideration of your Royal Highness we would always be very grateful.

　　Assuring your Royal Highness of our profound respect, we beg to subscribe ourselves;
　　　　your most obedient servants,

Alexr McDonald. Lui Ry Derry.
Alexander Grant. Mar Lodge.
John MacIntosh. Bynack.
Alexander Grant Geldie
Robert Lamont Geldie.
George Mitchell. Corriemulzie.

Request for wage rise by Mar Keepers

I found there were more adventures to be gleaned from those days: and within some letters from Captain Horatio Ross written in 1828 there is a record, as far as I can tell unpublished, of a bet for £2500.00. There had been a shoot at Blackhall in Kincardineshire, which belonged to Mr Farquharson. After they had been wading *in the morass* after duck during the day, a discussion resulting in a serious bet had taken place over which was the quickest way to Inverness: either to go on foot across the mountains or again on foot by walking the *coach road*. They appointed an umpire who was woken at 9pm after dozing off and asked to go with Lord Kennedy to Inverness by the route across the hills. He immediately agreed and set off. He left on record as follows... *I called to my servant to follow with my walking shoes and worsted stockings, and Lord Kennedy did the same. They overtook us after they had gone seven or eight miles. Fancy my disgust: My idiot brought us certainly worsted stockings, but instead of shoes, a pair of tight wellington boots: my language, I am afraid was more expressive than elegant. His excuse was that my shooting shoes were damp from wading in the morass in the day time: so that I had to make the best of it with the wellingtons. The sole of one boot vanished 25 miles from Inverness, and I had to finish the walk barefooted.*

A substantial snow Cornice 1930s

We walked all night, next day, and the next night-raining torrents all the way. We crossed the Grampians, making a perfectly straight line, and got to Inverness at 6 a.m. We never saw or heard of Sir A.L. Hay (he went by the coach road, via Huntly and Elgin, 36 miles further than we, but a good road) who appeared at 10 a.m., and who was much cast down at finding he had been beaten. I however told him that to the best of my belief he had won his bet..... Lord Kennedy, then a good deal beaten had leaned on the arm of his attendant in descending and ascending the hills.

Close up of Golden Eagle chick and a dead grouse

In the end Lord Kennedy and Sir Andrew Leith Hay decided between them to drop the bet while it was being referred to an expert on pedestrianism, Captain. Barclay. He told our narrator that he would have judged in favour of Hay, presumably because he had accepted no assistance.

Captain Barclay became famous for walking 1000 miles in 1000 hours over nearly six weeks. He won his bet of 1000 guineas by walking to a post and back on Newmarket Heath in 1809. He also won sustantial side bets.

Gleney

Donald McDonald was formerly head keeper at Invercauld, a great sprawling estate which marches with Mar Lodge. In his young day he was on Mar as a keeper. He was a great family friend known to many as Donald Bynack and spoke of the corrie in Glen Ey. *There is a great big stone hereaboot they called The Cailliache, aye well then this corrie is Clach Chaille and this aald keeper he said this it meant the Corrie of the Kale laddie. So I said there's nae kale there well he said if ever you are up go have a look at the lichen. So I went up and it was thick. There is* (also) *Meall Sgalan.* Meall Sgalan means lump of the sheltered place. There is an interesting place name away out Glen Ey called A' Mhoine Mairrneach, the Mar men's peat moss, where the folk of Mar used to go to dig for fir pine roots to use as fir candles, located towards Beinn Iutharn Mhor from Altanour. They would have been unlikely to have been given access to cut standing trees but would have had access to the moss where peat was cut and stacked to dry in the wind before being carted down to help sustain life in the winter time. When heading out the glen there is a place called Allt Clais Chail before you come to Altanour. This, Donald told us, means burn of the hollow of the kale, due to the resemblance to kale of the lichen. At Altanour, a cairn marks the grave of James McKenzie of Dalmore, Seumus Mor na Pluice as he was known in Gaelic, or James of the fat cheek, a man killed by caterans from Lochaber.

Donald continued; *My father's story wis that there wis a man Powel rented the shooting at Mar Lodge lang ago he wis a terrible wild kind o a customer he wis and he went abroad ye see to shoot some small birds for their feathers I think or fly hooks ye see or something and he took the head keeper wi him Ronald McDonald and of course I dinna ken what part o Africa it wis but oh he had any amount of money and had all the ponies and all the jewellry and he was giving the local inhabitants jewellry. And he was shooting these birds wi sparrowhail it was just a small gun they had not to mark them and they were all murdered but Ronald McDonald the Head keeper he told my father and he showed my father his jacket that this local wis after him nearly killed the whole rest o them and he ran and he held up this shield thing and he tried to get him here you see but he yelled and he got off and it was a missionary that saved Ronald McDonald he was the only one that wis saved. When he (the native) fired his (McDonald's) coat was waving and he showed my father his jacket and there was a hole right through it by dashed. He got clear! This missionary came on him and he was the only one that was saved with a hole through it. They say he was an awful wild man this Powell and he wounded a stag in this burn and he put the keeper up the keeper away after it Urquhart some of his people used to live up on Chapel Brae and he was taking a long time to get back and he wanted to get the stag to the top that wis the story and he was never comin back.* DM

The gun had discharged somehow and Urquhart was wounded: he died afterwards.

Corrour Bothy in the late 1920s or early 30s. It is located in the Lairig Ghru by the upper reaches of the River Dee at the foot of Devil's Point

Ian Grant mentioned the incident at another time; *There is a Cairn in the middle o the muckle Daviot oh aye that wis Urquhurt the keeper that shot himsel and Grant my grandfather was there at the time wi him when it happened he gaed awa aifter a wounded stag awa into the Eidiert somewye they dinna really ken exactly what happened he wisna deed I dinna think faan they got him, but he died on the wye and they left a man far the cairn wis.*

After one of my hill trips I found myself up at Ardoch speaking to Rob Bain when by we began talking about his relation Ronald McDonald. Rob told me that Ronald had gone on an expedition to Africa to Abyssinia whereby many

A' Chailleach, meaning the old woman, a stone left of picture in Glen Ey

of the expedition had been murdered by the natives. *Ronald McDonald got away by sheer speed of foot and walked and worked his way back through Europe* (not returning home for some months if not years.) *He came right up to the Derry Lodge where one of his relatives was heard to say: If I didna ken Ronald McDonald was dead I would've said that wis him comin up the drive, and it wis!*

I went to see Nell Bynack at her home in Braemar Her name was Nell McDonald but folk of the district often had by-names from their place of residences and Nell lived as a girl at Bynack lodge away out Glen Dee towards Glen Tilt. She was a sister to Donald McDonald, also known as Donald Bynack. *We had very enjoyable times ye know. There wasna many people wanderin the hills in those days. Across the hill two miles beyond Bynack was The March Burn, the Dooltin* (Dubh Alltan) *ye crossed hit and you were in Perthshire that was The Duke of Atholl's place ye crossed another hill a green hill and ye were into Fealar, Fealar lodge. I've done that too and my mother's done it with Donald* (Nell's brother Donald McDonald) *on her back. The keeper that was at Fealar Lodge there was three brothers on the Duke of Atholl's place and this*

The house called Mar Forest

Valuation of goods belonging to Angus McDonald Mar Forest Cottage Braemar November 29th 1899

Bedroom No 1	£	s	d
1 Mahogany chest of drawers	2	—	
1 " mirror		12	6
1 Towel rail		2	
1 dressing table		14	
1 wash stand		7	6
basin & chamber		3	
1 hair-mattress		15	
1 flock-mattress & chaff-bed		12	6
bed-curtains & counterpans		5	
Bedroom No 2			
1 deal chest drawers	1	10	
fender & tongs		2	6
2 pieces of carpet on landing		4	6
Parlour			
1 Parlour table	2		
1 couch	2	10	
3 hair bottomed chairs 15/-	2	5	
2 basket chairs 5/-		10	
2 folding chairs 3/-		6	
1 corner stand (inlaid)		12	
bamboo table, flower stand, & vase		10	6
carpet and 2 rugs	2		
fender and fire irons		9	6
curtain pole		3	6
6 pictures 3/-		18	
1 kitchen dresser	2		
chaff-bed & chamber		4	
wax-cloth in kitchen, passage, stair, and mat		7	6
1 towel rail		2	
coal shovel & 2 brushes		5	
1 glass decanter jelly-dishes and glasses		5	
dishes in kitchen		1	
1 ink stand		2	6
6 goblets, stewpans, boilers		18	
basin, soap-dish, nails, ladles and pans		10	6
4 facing-irons and devil		5	
lamp, knife-board, looking-glass, mantle-ornaments		5	6
Milk-house			
11 milk-basins, 1 cream jar, milk strainer		11	2
butter churn		3	6
Sundries 2 tubs 3/9		7	6
2 american axes 2/-		4	
1 box-barrow		15	
1 peat-barrow		4	
2 sythes 2/-		4	
shovel and spade		3	
3 hoes		2	6
1 fork		1	
2 grapes		2	6
1 rake		1	
1 cheese press and chisel		5	
2 washing pots		5	6
1 ton 3 cwt coals	1	17	
carried forward	32	5	8
171 yds: wire-netting	1	1	
378 yds: wood-fencing	1	11	6
	£34	18	3
To 115 ½ D. Day — @/10 £4.15.10			
36 Do — " — @/5 15			
	£5	10	10
	£40	9	1½

James McDonald Builder
John Ewan Builder

Paid Wm Thom
Angus McDonald
30/11/

List of possessions from resident at Mar Forest giving an insight into life at the time.

Ruins of Altanour Lodge at the head of Glen Ey

lad was the terribleist lad for drink that ever ye saw, he was aye drunk ye ken and he was warned and warned until at last there was a lad came up to see aboot the shooting ye see. He used to take the shooting, and the keeper was in the bed, so they couldna keep him any langer. My father went across one day (Nell laughs) *and he had a jar ye know wi a handle he had in alow the bed and a bowel to drink the whisky below the bed, so his wife afore my father gaed through to see him she says now daa taak onything fae him the day now she says because I've pitten caster oil in among the whisky. So faan ever my father gaed in he wis drove off into the bowel ye see. My father says I canna look at it the day noo he says I'm afa bothered wi an ulcer in my stomack the day. I just canna look at it the day! Faan my father next saw him he said, you kent fit wis in that whisky! He had the diarrhoea and had to go to the kirk and pit on the kilt. He was an affa man he wid go awa ower tae Fealar, through the nicht he wid say tae my mother and father awa tae yer beds and I'll rise faan its day licht. It wis dark it wis gettin nae day licht. He used tae taak my father's spring cart and horse and doon tae the village.*

I knew Nell would have known Seton Gordon so asked what she remembered of Seton, who had written some fine books on the area;

He stayed wi us a lot in the Derry when he was writing his books ye see. Him and his first wife: she dropped down wi a heart attack. She told me herself there had been a hide up in the Cairngorms (where they were) *watching the eagle and she told me that when she come oot o that hide she couldna stand. That wis Audrey, I've seen him comin to our place at Luibeg and* he *got the candle and the matches and he got his own room and at 3 o'clock in the morning away out at the snowbuntings. He was very interesting Seton Gordon, he used to go to Corrour Bothy in the winter time, blin drift, he stayed, him and a man Crue he had cancer o the face, he was quite well off this man wis. They had a well at Corrour faar they got the waater; and it was drifting like anything, wild; and he went away for the waater and he was never comin back that wis afore he got this bad face. So Seton thought he's nae comin back I'll play the pipes and he'll come back. That is what he said ye know. So next day, up and ower the back o Ben MacDui, (they went) it was a glorious day. It just shows ye how it can change ye know. Oh he stayed a lot in Corrour Bothy Seton Gordon. Thats far he did a lot o his writin. That is the place to meet people, in the glens: ye winna meet them here, leuch grunders (low ground) I caa them... Aa that ye see doon here is craaws. Ye dinna even here the Cuckoo doon here! The Cuckoo has arrived has it? There's anither bird that Seton told me aboot and thats the Sandpiper you will never hear them he said before the first or second week in April and he's dead right the 23rd or 24th of April (usually) so they have arrived too jist last week. The cuckoo! Dirty lazy brutes of birds! We had one at the Derry it laid its egg in a Heather Lintie's nest the peer little bird her eggs was thrown oot. Aifter the bird wis hatched anytime ye gaed in aboot the peer bird sat on top just like an umberella. I caa them lazy brutes. I never hear them doon here I never hear a bird I miss that terrible I was brought up in the country ye see up in the high Cairngorms. My father found a flare he was scared stiff it was a bomb ye ken he got it ower on the hill. It was dropped from a Zeppelin the folk o Mar Forest heard it. It made an afa queer noise a zeppelin, zoom zoom they were lost you see and they dropped this flare to let hem ken if they were ower water they were lost.*

We left Nell with the flare from a passing Zeppelin found by her father and her memories of the places which had made such a deep impression upon her, one of the last of her generation, and the folk of Mar Forest. She was less than content with the lower-ground residence and longed to be back at The Bynack away out Glen Dee. Away back to the glens with space and freedom to roam. "I come oot o a shootin lodge, ye ken", she told me, "nae a match box!"

THE FATAL RIFLE ACCIDENT IN MAR FOREST.— The following from the *Inverness Courier* is sent to us as a more correct version of this sad event:—"On Friday, the 5th inst., a fatal accident happened in Mar Forest, by which George Urquhart, the head forester, was killed. It appears that in the morning Mr. Powell, with Urquhart and another forester, named Peter Macintyre, went out deer-stalking on the face of Cairntoul, one of the highest of the Grampian range, on the ridge overlooking Glenglusechan. Mr. Powell, at about 2 o'clock in the afternoon, shot at and wounded a fine stag. Fearing he might escape by the pass he sent Urquhart, with a rifle, round the head of the glen, and the latter fired at the stag and again wounded him. John Grant, another forester, joined him, and they followed the stag, which was only able to go at a slow pace for about a mile down into a very steep burn, the sides of which rose precipitously for 200 or 300 feet. Being desirous to get the stag into more open ground before he killed him, Urquhart tried to drive him down the burn, pushing him with the butt end of the rifle. The stag, in his struggles, kicked the locks of the rifle, which were downwards, breaking the hammer of one lock off and striking the other hammer on to the cap, breaking the catch of the lock, and so exploded the rifle. The muzzle being pointed towards Urquhart's chest, the bullet went right through his side. The poor fellow stood for a moment, then, exclaiming, "I am shot," fell back into the arms of Grant, who was with him in the burn. Grant laid him down and did what he could to stop the bleeding; but Urquhart himself said he felt he was dying. Grant then ran to Glenglusechan to get the assistance of Mr. Powell and Peter Macintyre, who had in the meantime come round the head of the glen, and were waiting at the top of the ridge, unable to find out where Urquhart and Grant had gone to. They immediately went to where poor Urquhart lay, and Grant ran to the Geldie sheiling, one of the outlying lodges in Mar Forest, about seven or eight miles distance, for further assistance, and thence sent a messenger to Braemar, about 16 miles distance from the Geldie, for surgical assistance, and returned himself with the only other man at the lodge, Donald Fraser, taking with them a deer pony. In the meantime Mr. Powell and Peter Macintyre had been doing all they could to comfort and relieve poor Urquhart, who when they first came to him was perfectly sensible, and related how the accident happened, but after they had been with him about an hour he got much weaker, and died about half-past 5 o'clock. The stag which he had followed so keenly lay dead also in the burn within a few feet of him. It was about 7 o'clock before Grant and Fraser returned with the pony, and the body of Urquhart had to be carried from the burn to the top of the brae, and was then placed on the pony. By this time it was quite dark, and a dense mist came on. Mr. Powell and the three foresters very soon lost their way. The wind was in the east before darkness came on, and they hoped by keeping their faces to the wind to get to the Davy burn, and so on to the Geldie-lodge; but after walking for more than four hours they got into such broken and mossy ground that it was impossible to proceed further with the pony. It was perfectly dark, and they laid the body on the heather, expecting they would have to pass the night on the hill; but after proceeding some distance further and getting on to lower ground they saw a light, which proved to be a fire outside the Geldie sheiling, about four miles distant, and soon afterwards they met some of the other foresters, who had come out in search of them with a lantern. About 2 o'clock in the morning they reached the sheiling, where Dr. Marshall, of Braemar, and Dr. Maclaren, of Allan-a-quoich, were waiting. The body of Urquhart was taken home the following morning, and was to be buried on Wednesday last. The deceased was universally respected and liked by all who knew him. He was a most brilliant deerstalker, prompt in determining what course to adopt in following deer, and most successful in getting up to them. He was altogether as keen a sportsman as ever trod heather. The way he met with his death was certainly most extraordinary, for he may be said to have been shot by the stag he was pursuing."

A Canadian Diversion

The Second World War saw the arrival of the 25 COY Canadian Lumber Corps to Mar Lodge. They were mobilised at Fredricton in New Brunswick, arriving at Mar Lodge on the 30th of March 1942 and left the area on the 14th of June 1944. They had bases at several other places such as Abergeldie near Ballater. By chance, I was presented with some splendid pictures of their activities by Robbie Mitchell in Braemar, who went some way to researching them. I had written briefly in 1992 *In the Shadow of Lochnagar* of the Abergeldie camp. The Canadians seem to have been generally well received locally and kind to people, delivering firewood and the like. They installed their operations by diverting a stream from the River Lui and building a saw mill which was was located near the confluence of the Lui with the Dee and a bridge was constructed from logs across the River Dee and a railway was built to move the timber from the mill. They also installed a turbine upstream on the River Lui which provided the camp with electric light, which, I am told, was a novelty as it predated the electricity being installed to households locally. I met a chap John Stephen who was here at the time and he told me he had great memories as a boy when the Canadians were at Abergeldie because they provided such a fantastic Christmas party for the school children in one of their huts.

There is a much wider story which has been covered by others and some work has been done to highlight the Newfoundlanders' camp at Dalmochie near Ballater. It is important that this photographic record is preserved in book form. These photographs are of the Canadians' workings on the upper Dee.

The Canadians diverted part of the River Lui and made a channel where logs were floated along to a pond where they were cleaned of mud before being fed into a conveyor and then cut in their saw mill. A railway was installed to move the finished product: the engine would take timber across the log bridge over the Dee down to the roadside yard to be stacked. They were then trucked to Ballater station and then by rail to Aberdeen harbour. Part of Ballater's disused station is still sometimes locally referred to as the Canadian Bank where logs were loaded onto the train.

The log bridge over the River Dee built by the Canadians, was removed in the 1960s and had been badly damaged previously by flooding and ice.

Action shot as logs hit the water. The logs were offloaded into a channel leading to the log pond. This was done partly to remove mud and stones to prevent damage to the saws

Engine pulling planks from the mill across the River Dee

Offloading from a truck into channel leading to log pond

Canadian built bridge which survived until the 60s

Guiding logs onto a conveyor and into the mill

The sawmill which was located near the confluence of the Lui with the Dee

Bob Scott and Punch on the Derry road before Bob got a Landrover

December, 1916.

These Instructions cancel all previously issued except in regard to Routes.

COUNTY OF ABERDEEN.

Instructions to Civil Population in the Event of a Hostile Landing.

The following is the general sense of Government Instructions and Local Regulations in case of a Hostile Landing.

A landing is not considered either imminent or probable.

As, however, a landing is possible, the civil population should know what is required of them.

Orders will be given by the Police.

It is of the utmost importance that the movements of troops and artillery should not be hampered by the presence of numbers of civilians on the roads. It is therefore highly desirable that civilians remain in their houses except in the cases of heavy bombardments. If they move they should use the cart routes already arranged.

Civilians are liable for non-combatant duties, and able-bodied men must assemble to form working parties when, and where, ordered.

All Transport, viz.:—traction engines, motor cars, motor cycles, and bicycles (with any spare parts and tyres), horses, ponies, mules, and donkeys, carts, carriages, and other vehicles, surplus petrol, and harness must be removed along the cart routes already arranged, which must be rigidly adhered to.

Any of the above transport which you find yourself unable to remove should be destroyed when ordered. Should no special instructions be given, boats should be sunk or destroyed when ordered.

Any of the above transport and the following tools, viz.:—pickaxes, spades, shovels, felling axes, saws, and crowbars, and any rolls of barbed wire must be handed over to the military, as also arms and ammunition to the Police, if required.

Except in very exceptional circumstances, gas supplies in towns and villages should not be cut off.

Cattle, sheep, pigs, grain, and provisions are <u>not</u> to be removed or destroyed.

Carts, horses, and civilian traffic must in all cases give way to troops on the march by moving to the side of the road, or into the fields if necessary to clear the road.

To prevent congestion certain routes have been laid down for vehicles and persons accompanying them, of which due intimation has already been given.

Should anything in these instructions appear obscure, apply to your Special Constable for explanations.

[OVER

PROCEDURE.

On an Alarm being given by the Military or Police (including Special Constables)—

Read again carefully the above instructions.

HALF LOAD your carts or vehicles, including grain and one blanket or rug for each transport animal, and provisions and two blankets for each person accompanying the carts or vehicles.

> (It would be well to include a lamp or lantern with oil or candles, an axe or hatchet, pick and shovel, a bucket or pail, one or two cooking utensils, and for each person accompanying the carts, one plate, bowl, knife, fork, and spoon.)

Put in the carts or vehicles any FIREARMS or AMMUNITION, to be handed over to the Police.

> (Those not having transport available should arrange with the nearest owner of transport to remove same.)

Last of all, put in the carts or vehicles (preferably in a separate cart), any TOOLS, viz., pickaxes, spades, shovels, felling-axes, saws, and crowbars, and any rolls of barbed wire, for the use of the Military.

Harness horses, etc., and assemble surplus horses, ponies, mules, and donkeys that are to be driven off, and generally make all necessary arrangements so as to be in a position to comply with the above instructions immediately on receipt of orders to move.

Have ready duplicate lists of any property to be destroyed.

But note that no removal or destruction is to be commenced without orders.

On Receiving Orders to Move from the Military or Police (including Special Constables)—

Send traction engines, motor cars, motor cycles, bicycles, horses, ponies, mules, donkeys, carts, and other vehicles, and any people accompanying them, by the quickest way to join and follow the nearest of the Cart Routes, of which you have already been informed.

Destroy any spare harness and petrol which you are unable to remove.

Sink or destroy any boats in your possession, unless otherwise ordered.

Render useless traction engines, motor cars, motor cycles, bicycles, spare tyres, carts, and vehicles in your possession *which you find yourself unable to remove.*

CATTLE, SHEEP, PIGS, GRAIN, and PROVISIONS are NOT to be removed or destroyed.

On the Move—

Stick to the routes laid down for you, or you may find your vehicles, etc., jammed up by those from neighbouring parishes.

Follow all instructions given by the Special Constables, or their accredited assistants, of the parishes through which you pass.

NO REMOVAL OR DESTRUCTION IS TO BE COMMENCED WITHOUT ORDERS.

ABERDEEN and TEMAIR, Lord Lieutenant.

WM. SMITH, *Secretary,*
Central Organising Committee of the County of Aberdeen.

ABERDEENSHIRE LIEUTENANCY OFFICE,
CANADA HOUSE, 201 UNION STREET,
ABERDEEN, *December,* 1916.

56 OLD DEESIDE WAYS

Sunday 27th March 1955 Mr & Mrs R Scott & Punch Luibeg photo taken by Sandy Anderson

Chapter 5 **Ian Grant of Pinewood, Inverey**

Ian Grant was brought up in Mar Forest, where his father and grandfather had been keepers before him. Ian, it seems, had the run of the place and explored every nook and cranny. His nephew Ian Brown remembered going to his house for holidays and told me he was a quiet man and didn't really talk too much to them within the house: however, if they were out together fishing or on the hill, he would talk much more. He had the Gaelic and lived through a time when there were other Gaelic speakers in the vicinity growing up at the end of the road, so to speak. Most vehicles go no farther than Linn of Dee but the old ways spread out from there and beyond to Aviemore, Glen Feshie, Glen Tilt, glorious mountain passes. More subtly, the connections were among the folk, some of the Grant

Ian Grant at Corrour Bothy

family connections go back to Glen Tilt, which is hardly surprising. The old ways in this book refer to the ways through the hills but mainly the ways of life which are key. Alex Grant moved with his family from the house called Mar Forest to Luibeg in 1926. Alex and his son Ian worked as keepers from there. Alex retired to Pinewood, Inverey, in 1937. There were lots of folk going to the hills during that

A young Ian Grant playing the pipes at Luibeg

period and many of them stayed with the Grants at Luibeg, sometimes for the week, and Mrs Grant supplied them with bed and breakfast. The visitors' book of the period shows the enjoyable time those people had, made more enjoyable exploring the high Cairngorms and by a Highland family providing basic hospitality in such a grand location with Ian contributing to their enjoyment with his musical abilities: especially popular were his bagpipes. Adam Watson pointed out a place in the river where Ian Grant removed many tons of stones by Luibeg to form a pool in which he taught himself to swim.

I went to see Ian Brown, who remembered fondly his days with his uncle and aunt at Inverey.

Heading home by horse and cart

I just remember Ian Grant being a very shy chap and he didn't make conversation, if you asked him something, he would always show interest, particular if it was around local history, or wildlife or whatever. When my brother and I went up and stayed on our holidays when we were youngsters he would converse more with us if we were on the hill for a walk and fishing or whatever. I remember him saying they kept a pig when they were at Mar Forest and he must have been bored as a boy and made a whip started whipping the pig; the pig was squealing and squealing; his father turned the

Ruighe Ealasaid meaning Elizabeth's Shiel: note the grazing cattle

Ian Grant plays for mother and father at Luibeg

whip onto him. Ian died in 1980: auntie Wanie died the same year a few months earlier. He was born in Mar Forest in 1903 and became a keeper like his father although as a teenager I think he went for a season as a pony man or apprentice gillie at Ardverikie at Laggan he had also used to say he had gone and stayed with his Grandfather at The Red Hoose. I think that was John Grant that was Sandy Grant's father. Ian Grant's mother was Maggie Stewart of a family of Stewarts down Glen Tilt we have good records of that because her father was John Stewart known as Jock and her mother was a fluent Gaelic speaker and singer they were both born in the same year I think 1825 and from memory the father lived to 1896 but she lived on until the start of the first war. They were down Glen Tilt and her sons became keepers as well.

I asked Ian about the making of the spirit which I knew he had done. He didn't distil whisky until the 70s, Ian, though there was a recipe that his father had for making whisky... He dabbled in a lot of things. I went to see Robbie Mitchell in Braemar and he had some experience of Ian's whisky making.

Heavy snow fall

And then we gathered roon the blaze,
While Jock before us took his leisure,
And Ian played the pipes with praise,
And Mr Grant smiled round his pleasure.

And Mrs Grant, behind the scenes,
Was busy with her cooking,
As bright as if still in her teens,
And even more good looking.

When Ian got too old to manage I used to give him a hand with the hay and one thing and another I was invited in for a dram and he would aye come out wi a Balvenie bottle and it was a good dram and I got another ane but that was the extent o it, the two and it was comin up to New Year time and my wife said it'll have to be Balvenie so she went and got a bottle which wasn't to be opened until New Year, but an old friend came in so we cracked it open and I said: mighty, that's nothing like Balvenie but it says it on the bottle and it's nae been opened. It's nae near as good but it wisna until a while aifter. I micht have kent better because I was brought up at Lochnagar Distillery and the wife was in the village one day when someone asked: 'Is Robbie aye gettin a dram fae Ian?' 'Aye, Balvenie.' 'Balvenie my erse.' he said. 'That's his ain maakin.' Sometimes I'd go in (to Ian's house) *and there*

Thatched building, Inverey, in background

Salmon fishing guest

would be tubs sitting wi barley sprouting out of it. I would comment on it but Wanie aye said. 'That's Ian up to his beer makin tricks.' We lived directly opposite and I used to see smoke comin from this wee stone hoose (located) just next to their hoose. I said Ian must spend a lot of time in that wee stone Hoose. 'Och,' said Wanie: 'That's Ian makin oatcakes.' Lovat's father supplied the barley, the plumber made the still. Ian cut the peats and made the stuff (whisky) they must have been very patient to get that quality of stuff: it must have been distilled a lot of times.

Ian Brown continued…Ian ran the croft, kept three gardens and grew all his own vegetables to subsist on throughout the year and that included berry bushes, I remember having red and black currants and he kept bees; he made cheese from the cow. He had the cow right up until pretty close till the end. He had hens and ducks, of course, he collected his own firewood and cut his own peat. He liked to make things I suppose it was just that subsistence living and he read a lot. He was fascinated by other old trappers and people who lived in the wild and he made himself a pair of fur gloves for the winter out of skins from animals he trapped or shot. He didn't like heights particularly but he had a job to do up on the steading and he made a ladder out of a sapling tree which he cut down, he let it weather, he split it down the middle so that he had two 'D' shaped sides then he fitted rungs to it so he was quite adaptable in many *ways. Of course he had a great ear for music and he played piano accordion, fiddle and he played the pipes and to a good standard because back in the 50s Auntie Wanie was very good on the piano and they joined two others and made a local group which played for dances in the community hall in Braemar. Their pinnacle was that they once played on the Scottish dance music time radio and went into Aberdeen to be recorded. To travel into Aberdeen was an amazing event for these local folk that had hardly left the glen in their lives. Of course, he was a heavyweight athlete as well at the games and his father before him year on year at the games. He was*

Ian Grant with his pet owl

Alex Grant feeds deer with hay during winter

a good local champion which he won three years in a row here in Braemar. He wasn't in the same league as the major heavies at the time but a good local champion. Clark was one of the main ones at the time. He did horn craft and sold them to people who came: he was quite a talent and he had a fair collection of old guns that he had inherited: both sides of the families were keepers back to the 1800s so he had muzzle-loading guns. He would catch salmon after the war: of course there were plenty of salmon, then and through the war he would take fish, it was poaching but I think a lot of them were doing it but he was caught at the Linn o Dee after that he took them farther up the Dee or up the Ey. He would have had a deer when you have done it for the employer or the shooter but he only did that for food to see him through the winter. As they got older, some of the local keepers helped them a lot. Lovat Fraser was very good to them, he did a lot for them. I remember a keeper Ray coming in with a liver and a heart for them. Auntie Wanie had poured a dram for him, he turned green then white then said: 'Och that's grand!' It

68 OLD DEESIDE WAYS

On a stalk

IAN GRANT OF PINEWOOD, INVEREY

Ian Grant leads rescue from Derry Lodge team made up of keepers, his father is also in the group

was paraffin lamps that were lit at night and you went to bed with a candle or a lamp: they went out to milk the coo at night with a lamp. Ian always made his own oat cakes: there were several sheds outside. There was a stable, there was a byre, there was a peat shed and a stick shed and there was one that was kept locked. That was his workshop. He did his horn work there and he had a fire with a girdle and he made skirlie as well, from old recipes. It wasn't just salmon he caught; he would go up the Connie or the Cristie for the day; it was all worm fishing. When we were up on holiday we always had an expedition with him somewhere fishing. He told us about a deer watchers' bothy on the Dubh Gleann.

Lovat Fraser told me of Ian's whisky making adventures and that he made all his own ammunition. He added that after Ian died Lovat was clearing up the old shed and planned to burn it in the tidying up process. Ian had gunpowder tucked into various places which made an unusually fierce spectacular fire. Ian would occasionally go to the hill for a stag. Lovat told me they used to watch Ian through the binoculars. He had no rifle with him when he left but when he was up on the hill a rifle had manifested itself. He must have had one planted somewhere. He experimented with making his own whisky and the fact he distilled his own was occasionally whispered to me when taping the old residents. Lovat told me they were a real old traditional family living as they had done away into the past. I would have liked a news with Ian. It was inevitable he would find his way into one of these books as his name came up so frequently among the folk I have met and respect from the area. When interviewed for place-names, Adam Watson told me, Ian was probably the best informant over Mar Forest. He knew where Sergeant Davie's grave was, where Seamus Mor had been murdered by caterans and the stone of the lifting, Clach Thogalach in Glen Lui. Without this inquisitive nature detailed knowledge would probably have been lost. Lovat Fraser, Ian Brown and Robbie Mitchell all told me in similar ways individually that the Grants were an old old family living up there in a way that was becoming rare. I noticed they all smiled when thinking back to the days of one the upper Dee's old families and some of Ian's antics. More than once I heard fox-like used to describe his nature but in a complimentary empathic way. My favorite story on that concerns Old Mar lodge, if you will forgive me repeating a story I told in *The Dee From the Far Cairngorms* since I

IAN GRANT OF PINEWOOD, INVEREY 71

Feeding the deer at Luibeg

72 OLD DEESIDE WAYS

Returning from the Cairngorms with body slung across the pony's back

Working with hay for feeding the deer

Alex Grant with a fine stag

Luibeg 1932 with enclosed hayfield

Bob Scott of Luibeg, resident stalker in Glen Derry and well known to climbers and walkers of that time

now have photographs. Long ago the tenants of Mar Estate were all invited to Mar Lodge and asked to take their guns with them. They left their guns outside and went in to enjoy a celebration with plenty of whisky and food. When they finally came back outside, all their guns had gone. This had been a ploy to cut down on poaching on the estate. In subsequent years the entries in the Earl's journal seemed to indicate that he had some success with deer numbers increasing. Ian Grant's father had told him he could recall seeing piles of old guns lying up in the attic of Mar Lodge covered in dust and cobwebs.

Oh it wid hae been the first of the Duffs that came here or wid it hae been his son? It wid hae been between 1760 and the beginning o the next century. So he invited them a ower tae Mar Lodge, the whole lot o them and telt them tae bring their guns wi them ye ken. I suppose they thocht this wis a party. They were telt tae leave them ootside fan they gid in but faan they come oot the (the guns) wis awa. My father minded on the guns. They were awa up in the attic at the top o Mar Lodge there wid hae been aboot 60 o them, a the crofters' guns. It wid've been awa aboot the beginning o the century aboot 1800. IG

On 22nd August 1785 the Second Earl of Fife recorded in his hunting journal....*fine clear day hindered in the morning by seasing the arms of the people of Inveray which lands I have purchased at a most exorbitant price, to save my forrest from potchers.*

There is a long lineage in the Braemar area going back at least to Malcolm Canmore, (Ceann Mor in Gaelic) King of Scots. It is that of hunting the deer, a sport but of course necessary food for survival: later it meant jobs, keepering jobs, plus those of foresters, deer watchers and the like, giving stable employment not just in the shooting season but down the decades and centuries. It went a long way farther back than that, I have found skillfully worked flints which might go back eight thousand years. Therefore we can begin to see a pattern of man's relationship with the rivers and hills and glens of the area. They knew the hills intimately: sometimes several generations would stay on one part of this mountainous area, giving interesting knowledge in intimate detail, knowing the birds and animals which lived within it. That knowledge has dissipated now and often been lost through changing ways of life. An old gillie on the river will

Beatie, a tame stag at Luibeg

Alex Grant with telescope

tell you of where fish might be caught, behind a particular stone, in a particular pool with a particular fly under a particular sky in a particular height of water. The stalker, the farmer or forester have no less detailed knowledge of the land. There are still a few such as those left with long lineages. I say: listen carefully to what they tell you; some of the information in names and custom goes back centuries.

The Colonel's Bed (Leabaidh Choirneil) lower Glen Ey

Cascade on the Lui

Edward VII at New Mar Lodge

Duke and Duchess of Fife at Mar Lodge

Luibeg

Grant with young Golden Eagle

COLOUR PHOTOGRAPHS OF THE AREA

The Hairst near Ballater. Ian Murray

Ruins: Upper Glen Gairn looking towards Gairnshiel and Morven beyond. Ian Murray

Felagie, in the shadow of Creag Leek. Ian Murray

Weathered granite on Ben Avon. Ian Murray

COLOUR PHOTOGRAPHS OF THE AREA 85

A temperature inversion from Sron Riach on Beinn MacDhui, looking across the upper Dee to Cairn Toul, Sgor an Lochan Uaine (Angel's Peak) and Braeriach. Ian Murray

Low winter light and snow show up old run rig cultivations in Gleann Taitneach. Ian Murray

Lochnagar Spring Morning: painting by Howard Butterworth

COLOUR PHOTOGRAPHS OF THE AREA

Sandy Davidson's Cairn. Ian Murray

Lochnagar with a collapsed rockfall (from Parallel Gully B) lying across snow wreath. Ian Murray

Willie Findlay, Rob Bain, Willie Gordon, Jock Bain howing neeps in Glen Gairn

Wolves in Scotland: painting by Martin Ridley

COLOUR PHOTOGRAPHS OF THE AREA

Exploring a lochan

High lochan on Ben Macdui

Eagle over Sron Riach: painting by Martin Ridley

Chapter 7   **Howard Butterworth**

I watched Howard Butterworth work: he talked and painted simultaneously with ease. He was painting the opening ceremony of the salmon fishing season. Everyone had gone but I stayed to talk to Howard: he was quietly working away on the opposite bank from where the opening ceremony had taken place. From the scene across the river, I watched him skilfully work his brush: trees emerged, people, sky and river.

This is the fourth coat of paint, he said. I asked if it was possible to paint too much: how did he know when to finish a painting?

I am going to name drop now, laughed Howard *The Queen Mother had a seriously good eye for a painting,* he told me, *she could look around a room and point and say 'that is the one.' She could easily have been a serious artist. I saw a drawing she did when she was very young. She told me that Augustus John had great difficulty knowing when to stop when painting pictures: his family used to take his paintings off the easel to stop him painting more. So I said 'this one is overworked is it, maam?' 'Just a bit' she said.*

First lamb by Howard Butterworth

There's some amazing detail emerging, I said as I watched. *A lot of it is observation and the other thing that is happening is that I am moving trees and things, it's not exactly as it is.*

Howard came to Glen Muick in the 1977 with his wife, Hilary, and there they raised a family of Sarah and Mary-Louise and son John Paul, while his beautiful paintings emerged over the years. He still produces and I enjoy a coffee with Howard; we look at life through our different perspectives: it's refreshing. *When we came to Glen Muick it was 1977. Sir Ian was the Laird. We could see the hills from the front of the cottage and there was a minimal amount of traffic on the roads. We didn't get coach loads of people looking into the house which is the current situation in Glen Muick. There is a story that I feel obliged to tell which is that the Queen Mother helped my friend to control a bull at one*

Fraser's Brig, Glen Clunie near Braemar by Howard Butterworth

Howard paining by the River Dee Potarch

of the fields at the bottom of Glen Muick. He was trying to get it to go somewhere else and it wasn't having it but she suggested he go and get its mother and it worked. It was the Queen Mother's idea: she just happened to having a walk.

Things changed in Glen Muick about the time the Ford Sierra changed to the Ford Mondeo, he told me: that extra 15 mph meant life became a bit quicker. *There is a spirit in Glen Muick,* he says, *a female she's here just now. There is a place up there where you get a very strong idea that someone is watching you.*

I like the birches in Glen Muick especially the pendulous variety that hang so elegantly in the air. Howard is best known for his silver birches and expert at painting them.

It's taken me a long time to paint a birch tree properly, he says modestly, *if you put too much detail in, it doesn't look right.*

Howard painting by the River Dee, September 2015

Reluctant Spring, by Howard Butterworth. The Aald Brig of Dee

I made a very famous friend in Perth. I met Victor Spinetti, the film star and friend of Richard Burton and Elizabeth Taylor and goodness knows who else. He said something very important to me. We were discussing what we were doing with our lives and he asked me what I did and I told him that I was a product manager involved with plastic pipes and he then said: 'Ah but what do you want to do?' And I said paint pictures: then he said the magic phrase which I am passing on now to whoever reads this: Who is stopping you? It's such a wonderful phrase: it's always easier not to do something no matter what it is. Anybody who does anything worthwhile has to work at it.

I was brought up as a battery hen in Rochdale where you were expected to get a job and work in a factory. The farmers in Huntly, where Howard stopped before coming to Deeside, was a great stepping stone because they were much more independent and self-employed. *Being an artist has never been easy financially but you are free.* His sister encouraged him to paint and when he was working full time for a company he was conscious that his children were growing up not knowing him so it was a good reason to change. *The best one-liner I got over the phone was when I phoned this company and said: 'Good morning, sir, I am your new rep'. 'That is your bad luck, son, why are you phoning me to tell me about it'?*

I had noticed that certain photographs or paintings gave a pleasant feeling of satisfaction as well as just a pleasant scene. Howard had this to say.

Rapid Eye Movement when people are feeling relaxed they go into a state where there is rapid eye movement even when they are asleep and this is a deeply relaxed dream-like state and it's my contention that as an artist, if you are an artist and you can induce rapid eye movement then it works the other way round so if you have a painting that makes you move your eyes about looking at it, makes you feel good. So, for my own personal pleasure, I automatically do paintings that give rapid eye movement so I think that is definitely part of my success. I don't have to paint for the public: I paint for me. I genuinely think that is one of the things.

The Chinese have a saying that the best one is six. The sixth is the best one if you are painting something then after that it gets worse, I wouldn't put a figure on it myself but you do get better.

As I walked away I looked back at the artist fully in his element and saw suddenly the picture come together. 'How's it looking?' he asked. 'Perfect,' I replied! Howard's paintings are forever part of Deeside and its ways. I left the master to his craft.

Chapter 8 **Paul Anderson**

A tradition of fiddle playing goes back a long way in the area's history, many tunes played the world over can be traced back to notable fiddlers such as James Scott Skinner of Banchory and Peter Milne of Tarland.

Paul Anderson has taken these playing careers with him on his journey but also composed a great many tunes of his own. So where did this journey with the fiddle begin? I was curious to know

We wound the clock back nearly forty years to when Paul and his brother David were staying at their grandparents' house and had been put to bed. They were supposed to be sleeping but found it much more fun to have a look under the bed and in a chest of drawers, where among other things, a box containing old postcards was kept. They quietly pulled that out with some other items so they could look at the old pictures. One of the treasures they pulled out was a case containing a fiddle. For a while thereafter as a wee boy when visiting granny, Paul would disappear

Paul Anderson with Dougal on first visiting Ballochbuie Forest

Paul Anderson on the bank of The River Dee, Poll nan Sleac (pool of the slabs) 2015

to where the violin was kept, the family wondering what he was up to. He would then give little performances to the family at some point: later he went to granny and said he would like to learn to play. She told him she would let him have the fiddle if he went for lessons. Paul today plays the same fiddle which has gone with him on many trips abroad including many US States. It has been his instrument of choice nearly all of his career as a professional traditional fiddler.

Granny wanted a fiddle in the hoose. There were often unplanned ceilidhs at Granny's where folk would sing or tell a story or play the fiddle so she had wanted a fiddle in the house for such occasions. A relation of granny's was selling a fiddle for ten shillings, which my granny paid: it's a French fiddle, it's a good instrument. There was a wee bit of a fiddle tradition in the wider family. There has been a lot of effort and tuition between then and now.

Paul named many whom he admired as players and his teachers who helped him on his way.

I wid hae been aboot 5 but aifter we heard the sitting room door close we were in the chest of drawers: there were suitcases and one of the things was a fiddle case with this aald fiddle. Once we had discovered it and we were at Granny's I would be upstairs scraping away on the fiddle: to my mind I was playing it but I wasn't playing notes just open strings. The fiddle was far too big for me at that age. I forgot about it for a while and took a notion to play the bagpipes, Dad had LPs which I liked, especially the Corries. A lot of the songs are about which tied into the turbulent times in Scottish history. Father read Kidnapped to me and these stories about the Red Fox made an impression. I can vaguely remember seeing someone on the TV playing the fiddle which I thought was amazing so at that point I went to granny and said I'd quite like to learn to play, so the fiddle was sent away to get sorted up. I started at Tarland primary school with Andy Linklater for a short period. I played a 3/4 fiddle then. The first concert would have been the school Christmas concert playing with some of the other kids, which I found quite terrifying and froze and was miming. The following year, I mind Dad asking me if I would like to go to the Banchory Strathspey and Reel Society junior section? So I went there then started going to fiddle competitions. The Strathspey and reel societies kept things going through the 50s 60s and 70s cultivating the fiddle when it was less popular at the time. They had some really good fiddlers which pulled you on and also having folk your own age playing as well was great. I was never gifted academically, never good at maths as an example but finding I could pick up the fiddle quickly felt great and the Scottish music just clicked for me. I won my first competition when I was ten. It might sound like I am blowing my own trumpet but I did seem to have an aptitude for it. The second ane was at Kirriemuir Angus Fiddle Festival: it was a big class aye a very good competition fiddlers from Edinburgh and Inverness, North East, winning it was a great thing. Alistair Hardie was one of the judges. Alistair came from a long line of fiddlers and makers and one of his ancestors was Mathew Hardie who was known as the Scottish Stradivarius: they are excellent instruments which are worth a lot of money.

As I spoke to Paul he had completed writing his Hielan Symphony, twenty five minutes of music in four movements.

They are all quite distinctive, he told me, it is very Scottish in character but I did want the basic melodies to be able to be played by a traditional fiddler as well. Some of the more classical music you hear now is very clever but it doesn't do it for me: I need a tune. There is a historian called Ron Brander and he spotted the name The Hielan Man's Road on the edge of an old map. So we decided to call it The Hielan Symphony. My interpretation is it's more than just one road: I took it to be the whole network of the roads the journey starts at Huntly and finished at Falkirk. So that is what inspired it. I came up with the main musical line and my wife Shona worked with me on the keyboard to find the chords I was looking for.

The thing is: describing Paul's playing is about as easy as trying to describe a winter walk on Ben Avon to someone: ideally you have to be there, listen to the man play if you get the chance, he has carved a career as a professional traditional fiddler in his own way with the roots of his music deep into the past. Living and breathing the Howe of Cromar and the surrounding area, his beloved homeland. Moreover, he has contributed by keeping alive that fiddle tradition in the area which is thriving, I believe, in no small manner due to himself and his family and musical friends. He is also a valued adjudicator.

From the left back, Shona Donalson, Alistair McDougal, front author, Matt Milne, Paul Anderson taken at Naul whilst on musical tour in Ireland

When you lay out your own work on an album it's like baring your soul he said once whilst we were walking on the hills around Ballater. *What's the difference when you are writing?*

One difference is there is no applause when you produce a book, I laughed.

I went to the first playing of his symphony one evening in Tomintoul, there was huge applause and little wonder. Since then I have enjoyed listening to its second airing with a larger orchestra at Aboyne theatre. I hope this will just be the start for The Hielan Symphony.

I'm nae Beethoven, says Paul, but it consists of 25 minutes of music in symphony's in four movements.

Paul has a few strings to his bow, he composes, teaches fiddle, has produced several CDs and is a successful performer. His life revolves around music and music revolves around him and his wife Shona Donaldson's beautiful singing voice. Brother David and sister Heather are accomplished fiddlers, his cousin Gary plays accordion and three of his nieces play.

Not bad from a fiddle found below a bed, I said. It makes complete sense as the generations move forward and the music with it. Some things should carry forward, we need our torch carriers.

Apart from myself my brother David and Heather play, my cousin Gary plays accordion and Averil his sister and my cousin plays fiddle and my three nieces play Eilidh, Rhiann and Katie.

There is a musical link directly to Neil Gow, the father of Scottish fiddle music through his fiddle teacher. Although my classical teacher was Andy Linklater who was the school violin tutor, I received private fiddle lessons in the Scottish fiddle idiom, first from Angus Shaw of Banchory and then Douglas Lawrence. Douglas was taught by the legendary Hector MacAndrew. Hector was taught by his father who was in turn taught by his father Peter, a native of Dunkeld who was taught by James Macintosh, the last pupil of Niel Gow.

His notes and compositions resonate from the fiddle in the present day but also from deep into the area's past. One man's living passion can and should influence and inspire also into the future. Paul is carrying forward a strong line of tradition for others to aspire to but is also blazing his own trail with his own compositions and style: from him, fellow fiddlers and his pupils, the future of the craft is more secure. I feel, although he as achieved a lot, we will be hearing much more from him and the fiddle he found below the bed. More power to your bow, Paul.

Chapter 9 *Burn o' Vat*

The Burn o' Vat in spate August 2015

Issued by the Privy Council 1636. *Patrick Macregor and others hes associat and combynned themselves togidder, hes thair residence neere to the forrests of Culblene, Glentanar and in the mountains of Tullich, Strathdie, Glengarne, Strathdone and Cabrach, and from these parts they come in darknes of the night down to the incountrie, falls unawars upon the houses and goods of his Majesties poore subjects and spoyle theme of thair goods, and, being full handed with the spoyle they goe back agane to the bounds forsaids where they keepe mercat of thair goods peaceablie and uncontrolled to the disgrace of law and justice. For the remeid whairof the Lords of Secreit Councell charge all landlords and heretours, where thir brokin lymmars has thair resset, abode, and to hunt, follow, and persew the saids theeves, and never to leave aff their persute till they be ather apprehended or putt out of the countrie.*

McGregor was hanged in 1658. Local folklore states he once avoided detection by hiding behind the waterfall within the open cave of the Vat.

Whatever the McGregors were up to in these parts, it makes for interesting reading and folklore I remember my first visit to the Burn o' Vat as a child being all the more magical because of the mention of Rob Roy who we were told, once was there. The cave is still often referred to as Rob Roy's cave after Rob Roy McGregor who is buried at Balquhidder, surely one of the most famous Mcgregors. However, it does seem more likely that the lesser-known name of Gilderoy's Cave is the more accurate referring to the above Patrick McGregor or his kinsmen. Rob Roy could

The old drovers' route looking back towards Marchnear

have been there and it is a dangerous thing to speculate and rule out tradition. For example Grant in his *Legends of the Braes o' Mar* mentions Sir Walter Scott's novel *Rob Roy*. *Rob was, it seems sent by the Earl of Mar in 1715 to raise the arm-bearing men of a portion of the clan seated principally on Gairnside.* Glen Gairn or Gairnside is a short distance from the Vat, especially on horseback. If the connection with Rob Roy is a myth, this may be its source. Another connection with that event was the Earl of Mar's Breakfast Stone. Sir Alexander Ogston provided some key folklore in his volume *Antiquities of Cromar*. He talks of The Earl of Mar; *The legend being that he had his morning meal after the raising of the standard of Rebellion at Braemar in 1715, on a large slab lying at this spot.* The stone was located by the old drove road from Marchnear to Tullich. He goes on to say that the stone was broken up by masons for building material. Interestingly, a small hillock still retains the name but I have heard no one today refer to it as the Earl Mar's hill. *A small conical hill, 100 yards distant, and 30 degrees west of north of the stone.* The danger of no known significance being attached to something like that can mean it was regarded as just a stone and so, when roads and buildings were made, the custom was to use what was lying close by. Large rocks were often used for lintels above the fireplaces, door or windows. By many old buildings it is possible to walk into the hills beyond and find stones with drill holes where they have been cut. Another historical loss to local folk was the Market Cross at Tullich which was *dinged doon* and put into the bridge.

The statistical account of 1794 gives a good description of the Vat at that time.

In the fore mentioned hill of Culblean, there is a moſt remarkable hollow rock, which, from it's ſhape, bears the name of Vatt, and through which a rivulet runs. In going up to visit this natural curioſity, a stranger is much ſtruck with the narrowneſs of the entry to the Vatt (being leſs than an ordinary door) and the large ſpacious area in which he immediately finds himself encloſed by rocks from 50 to 60 feet high, and from the fiſſures of which tall and healthy birch trees are growing. There is one particular clift of the rock which the eagle generally occupies as a ſafe and ſecure aſylum for hatching and nouriſhing her young, and where her nest is always to be seen. The rivulet falls down at the upper end through broken ſhattered rocks, and when flooded adds greatly to the pictureſque appearance of the whole.

The Kinord Cross, in itself still a statement of former people

The Vat is an ice age legacy shaped by rocks tumbling under pressure inside to form the open cave-like feature from melting glaciers. The floor is of red granite gravel and when standing inside we are probably standing many feet above the actual base of the cave approximately half way up.

It was Bill Gillanders who took me to see Annie Gordon at Dinnet: She had been brought up at The Coldrach *richt at the fit o Craig Nordie* west of Crathie before moving to the Kinord area. We went up the lane at Dinnet

Aerial photograph by author showing Loch Kinord with Castle Island (larger of the two islands) and The Crannog, the small island below right of centre. Culblean Hill beyond

and met her in the upstairs of her home. She was pleased to tell me of her time as a girl growing up at Aberarder school. The reminiscences I placed in my first book *In the Shadow of Lochnagar*. Now I am writing on the Kinord area I find her other anecdotes relevant in showing some of the beliefs the folk had. *There was a water Kelpie in Loch Kinord,* she stated, *they taen the bridle aff o' it. It used tae hing in the barn at Waterside. They say that wis richt enough lang ago, ye ken!* Of Ratlich, a former farm in Aberarder, she stated simply; *They say the Deil wis seen at Ratlich!*

I did not find any other superstition and she was always factual, so assume there must have been a primitive belief concerning a Kelpie on Loch Kinord. Is that worth preserving? We don't believe in Kelpies these days, but a grand thing to keep the bairns back from the boggy holes, I think, or a discussion point on a Sunday afternoon walk! The Water Kelpie was believed to take the form of a horse. Loch an Oir near Loch Builg in Upper Glen Gairn was said to be guarded by a water Kelpie: this is one of several instances in folklore I have come across a Kelpie mentioned on Upper Deeside. When the mist was on the water and darkness fell, superstition was intensified away back. Ronnie Robertson once told me of a man who came across from Fealar Lodge and was terrified at an apparition which the old keepers called the Will o the Wisp. His dogs barked in the gloaming at this dancing apparition which seemed to emanate from the Bog Myrtle. Most likely gas from the bog. Lochs Kinord and Davan, with its many birds and mammals had plenty to spook the walker at dusk. In

The huge cauldron of The Vat

the days when the horse was on every farm in the area and sometimes an old horse was deliberately drowned, it is little wonder the Water Kelpie has popped up fleetingly in the folklore. When Patrick Davidson was converting buildings to a home at Balgairn near Ballater he found the skulls of horses carefully inserted below the floor by some person many decades earlier.

> I'm feared o' the road ayont the glen,
> I'm sweir to pass the place
> Whaur the water's rinnin' ,
> far a' fowk ken
> there's a kelpie sits at the fit o' the den,
>
> And there's them that's seen his face
> But whiles he watches an' whiles he hides
> And whiles, gin na wind manes,
> Ye can hear him roarin' frae whaur he bides
> An' the soond o' him splashin' agin' the sides
> O' the rocks an' the muckle stanes.
>
> Violet Jacob

Spagnum moss was gathered locally, dried and sent to the Front in the first and second world wars as field dressings, its antiseptic and highly absorbent qualities making it ideal for treating the wounded soldiers. There is an area marked on the maps as Keiselguhr: this was where diatamite was mined and used in the manufacture of dynamite. Willie Downie of the Level told me that his uncle had worked there and taken some home, where it was found ideal for cleaning silver.

The Burn (stream) of Vat rises on Culblean Hill, runs through the open cave of the Vat and into Loch Kinord. The other loch, Davan, lies in close proximity to Kinord, draining water from Cromar.

Grant mentions; *Before parting with Malcolm Canmore, let me add a few words more. Some years ago a party of excursionists, boating on Loch Kinnord, drew out from near the larger island a log of oak bearing 1113, a date only twenty years after Malcolm's death. Great quantities of huge beams of oak, many tennoned and morticed, (perhaps the remains of a bridge) have been drawn out at various times, but no other having any inscription.*

Some of this oak was taken to build the foundations of the first Ballater bridge over the River Dee.

We fished on nearby Loch Davan as a family when I was a boy with permission from the tenant at Glen Davan House. The right to father to fish came with conditions: teach your sons to fish, and never take the boat out. The boat was a fascination: it was a very old weathered wooden boat inside an old boathouse with a rusted padlock and chain. There had been a drowning from it in the Thirties and so the vessel remained unused. We had great harmless fun fishing in the summer evenings: when it became a reserve they stopped people from fishing there. One evening, we found the hilt of an old sword but, sidetracked by the excitement of fishing or darkness coming down, we managed to go home without it. Not that it is terribly significant, this would have been in close proximity to the ancient Hall of Logie-Rothwayne used by Andrew de Murray's army the evening before the Battle of Culblean. Sandy Milne, a great family friend, used to tell me about fishing there from the boat in the 1940's casting with a

The Burn o' Vat in past times covered in graffiti

fly rod into the reeds. He recalled catching a pike with a large lump in its belly which turned out to be a rat. That put him entirely off eating his catch or any in the future. Unravelling history from what we find lying around the moor is a pleasing pastime. I was shown the Four Lords' Stones some years ago by Bill Gillanders and Ronnie Robertson. They are four naturally occurring stones significantly like the Earl Mar's Breakfast Stone lying by the old drovers' route across the moor from Loch Davan to near Tomnakeist which was once known as the Old Ballater Road. Place names are great preservers of history, like invisible bench marks on the hill side. The folklore associated with them was that four lords had dined there before a battle. So if the four lords existed who were they, likely to have been? The Four Lords' Stones have been nagging loose ends. Satisfied that the name and perhaps for the first time, picture to go with it means they won't be overlooked has left the interesting question: while I realise I can never prove their use, I have previously found folklore from the old families too accurate and interesting to ignore.

Chapter 10 *Battle of Culblean*

As the reader and possibly walker explores, it may be worth pondering firstly the Battle of Culblean, fought on the land nearby in relatively close proximity to the stones on 30th November 1335. Also The Race of Tullich, where it seems a much later battle took place. My thinking is that the Four Lords' stones hark back to folklore associated with one of these events but also I have noticed features near old routes across the moors and glens very often have names to them, especially prominent stones.

It's difficult to research history like this without wanting to get bogged down in the Battle of Culblean. The battle is a whole subject unto itself which is fascinating still, many centuries on, historians debate it, I found little folklore on Culblean, probably because most of my informants were farther up the Dee Valley but also the battle was so far back in time. This is in contrast to Culloden, concerning which I was still able to pick up unpublished folklore from reliable families who had been in the area since the 1700s.

The Clashneach (hollow of the horse) Boulder, on the left of picture, Ronnie Robertson (centre) and Bill Gillanders (right) show IM.

One piece of folklore that has arisen in conversation several times was that the Red Burn was so named because it ran red with blood I heard the same story about The Bleedy Burn. Usually with folklore it is my experience that stories handed down through reliable local old families hold some truth and if not at least I can record the beliefs at the time. There are other red burns in the area: in Gaelic Allt Dearg as an example on the side of Loch Muick translates as red burn; the sand and rocks on the side of it are very obviously red from a red granite colour. The Burn of Vat itself would certainly be a red burn with very red sand. The red burn currently named was also known as the burn of Logie from Alltan Lagaidh west of Loch Davan: a house in close proximity retains the name. On inspection the burn is literally red from the granite sand so the name may be a reference to this rather than blood. I don't doubt though a burn in the vicinity could turn red with blood as they are pretty small streams and killings are mentioned within a ford. Also the following quote from De Wyntoun states in a roundabout way that there was bloodshed within a pool of water.

Schyr Eobert Meyhneis till Canmore
Went, qwhare he wonnand wes before:
Thiddyr he went, and in a pele
He sawffyt hym and his menyhe welle.

More significantly perhaps are the lines;

Thai straweht tharein relation speris,
and thai thaim mete
In to **the fwrd**. *Eobert Bradey,*
Ane hardy knycht, thare gert thai dey.

So the ford as well as giving a clue to location also may have run red with blood.

Culblean, to put it in context, came not long after Bannockburn, was won in 1314, and, as I write, has just celebrated its 900th anniversary. W. Douglas Simpson, a noted historian, writes in 1931:

Popularly it is supposed that the struggle for Scottish independence was decided, once and for all, on the field of Bannockburn 1314. No greater misreading of history could well exist. The Treaty of Northampton, which closed the First War of Independence, was not signed until 1328; fourteen years of weary bloodshed remained yet after Bannockburn.

BATTLE OF CULBLEAN

Kildrummy Castle ruin, photographed around 1880, which was under siege just prior to The Battle of Culblean in 1335

The Scottish King Robert the Bruce died in 1329. This was the year 1335. Strathbogie had laid siege to Kildrummy Castle, which is not far from our area of interest. A plea for help was sent out to Andrew de Murray, Warden of Scotland, from Dame Christian Bruce, who was both sister to the late king and wife of Andrew de Murray. He set forth in haste, arriving on the scene with, according to our main source, 800 men on horse. Strathbogie meanwhile had heard they were coming, lifted the siege on Kildrummy and had made his way as far as Culblean. The battle site has been the subject of debate among scholars for a long time or would have been had they existed at the same time. A large stone erected by the Deeside Field Club sits on the moor commemorating the battle. It summarises the event as follows;

Ronnie Robertson at The Four Lords' Stones

BATTLE OF CULBLEAN 1335
ERECTED BY THE DEESIDE
FIELD CLUB IN 1956, TO COMMEMORATE
THE BATTLE OF CULBLEAN FOUGHT ON
ST.ANDREW'S DAY, 30TH NOVEMBER 1335. BETWEEN
THE FORCES OF SIR ANDREW DE MORAY, WARDEN
OF SCOTLAND, AND DAVID, EARL OF ATHOLL, IN
WHICH THE FORMER WERE VICTORIOUS. THE BATTLE
MARKED THE TURNING POINT IN THE SECOND WAR OF
INDEPENDENCE.
ADD GLORY TO THE PAST

Historians have gone over the battle in detail but they all refer to one common source and that is Andrew of Wyntoun's Orygynale Chronicle. With that in mind, I was soon drawn into the text. He lived from 1350 to 1425. His detailed account mentions at times individual features of this area in which the battle took place. My interest here is to understand the text he has left us and preserve the small amount of folklore surviving. His version as close as I can get to is written in an old form of Scots.

BATTLE OF CULBLEAN 115

WHEN" Schyre Andrewe off Murrawe herd,
How rudly the Eril Dawy ferd
Wyth his men, he wes all angry,
And thoucht to rays the sege in hy.
Than all thame gaddryd he,
That on sowth-halffe the Scottis Se
He mycht purches off armyd men :
The Eril Patryke come till hym then:

Wyth hym bathe Ramsay and Prestown,
And othir sere off gret renowne;
Willamo off Dowglas als wes thare
Wytli his gud men, that worthy ware,
And othir sere, qwhill thai war then

Welle aucht hundyr off fychtand men:
The floure off that half the Scottis Se
At that tyme in his Court had he.
Thai rade on thare way sa fast,
Qwhill thai have the Mownth sawffly past.

The Eril herd off his cummyng welle,
And departyde swa fra the castelle:
Till Kylblene strawcht the way tuk he,
And lugyd thare hys gret menyh
At the **est end**, *rycht in the way.*
And rycht befor thame, qwhar thai lay,

Earl Davy heard Murray was coming and left the castle moving to Culblean, taking his many troops to the east end, camping in the middle of the old road.

At the Halle off Logyrothwane
Schyr Andrew his herbry has tane.
Syne come till hym fra Kildrwmy
Thre hundyr, I trow wycht and hardy,
That comfort his men [a] gret thyng;
And he wes glade off thare cummyng.

So in his cumpany wes ane
Jhon off the Crag, that [liade] bene tane
Wyth the Eril, and suld his rawnsown pay
Apon the morne, that wes his day :

Murray and his men settled at Logierothwayne, which is located on the east edge of Loch Davan. They were greatly cheered by the arrival of 300 men from Kildrummy. From there are views across the loch to Culblean. The old moat is clearly visible to this day once the eye is in and would probably still contain water from the nearby marsh had a channel not been cut in it to allow it to drain.

He sayd to the lordis in prewate,
Gyve thai wald trow his cownsalle, he
Suld throw the wode a redy way,
Enwerown quhare thare fays lay
And behynd, bryng thaim on welle nere,
Or thai owcht off thaire cummyng suld here.
And he fullfillyd all, that he hycht;
Eor swne efftyr the mydnycht
To Dey he led thaim, and thare thai
Fand in the wode a redy way:
That way thai went, qwhill that thai ware
Passyd thare fays a mylle and mare.
Endlang the wode war wayis twa;

Culblean Memorial Stone

Murray divided his men into two parties. One column under the command of Douglas advanced towards the Atholl Army whilst the other column under Murray took a more indirect route leaving some time after midnight and guided by John of the Craig, who had detailed knowledge of the land.

The Eril in the **umast** *lay off tha:*
The Scottis men held the **tothir way***;*
Syne owrthort to that way held thai.
Thare hors thai levyd thare ilkane,
Syne to thare fays on fut ar gane,
That off thare come wyst nakyn thyng.
Bot syne welle swne in the dawyng

Thare dyscuverouris gat on thaim sycht,
That wyth all hy, that evyr thai mycht,
Warnyt the Eril ; and he in hy
Gert trwmpe, and warnyt his cumpany:
And thai till hym assemblyd swne.
In till schort tyme so have thai dwne,
That **at a lytill peth***, was thare,*

All sammyn thai assemblyd ware.
Evyn in the peth wes Eril Davy,
*And till **a gret stane**, that lay by,*
He sayd, " Be Goddis face, we twa
The flycht on us sail samyn ta."

Willame off Dowglas, that had then
*The **waywarde wyth** the wychtast men,*
That ware in all thare cumpany,
Qwhen that he sawe the Eril Dawy
Stand wyth his men arayid swa,
Hys spere in bathe his handis can ta
And kest it owrthort, and can say,
*" Standis **lordis** a stownd;" and thai,*

Seeing the small amount of men before him David Earl of Atholl, mistook the skilled movements to entice them to attack as fear on the part of Murray's. *For thai ar welle nere discumifyte.*

That war in till his cumpany,
Murmuryde tharoff all prcwcly.
Qwhen the Eril [Dawy] saw, that thai
Stwde swa, in hy he brak aray,
And cryid, " I ley ! apone thame tyte,
For thai ar welle nere dyscumifyte."
Than till a fwrde downe can thai ga :
And qwhen the Dowglas saw thaim do swa,
He sayde, " Now we." But mare lete,
Thai straweht thare speris,and thai thaim mete
*In to **the fwrd**. Eobert Bradey,*
Ane hardy knycht, thare gert thai dey.
Amang thaim strakis gret thai gave.

Andrew de Murray then, to the surprise of the Atholl men then in from the flank sturdily pushing down bushes in their way.

Wyth that Schyr Andrewe off Murrawe
Com in on syd so sturdely
Wyth thame all off his cumpany,
That in thare cummyng, as thai say,
Thai bare down buskis (bushes) *in thare way.*
Fra he assemblyde abade nane;

*The comownys all the flycht has tane.
Thare by an ake deyd Erie Dawy,
And syndry off his cumpany :
Schyre Waltyr Cwmyn als wes slayne;
And Schyre Thomas Brown wes tayne;
That syne wes hevyddyt hastily:
It semyd thai luwyd hym noucht grettumly.
Schyr Eobert Meyhneis till Canmore
Went, qwhare he wonnand wes before:
Thiddyr he went, and in a pele
He sawffyt hym and his menyhe welle.*

They fought and Murray, Warden of Scotland was victorious. Casualties the chronicles tell us were light with many soldiers under the English regime running off into the woods.

*And syne apon the tothir day
He tretycl, and come to thare fay.
Thare war bot fewe slayne in that fycht,
For the wode held thame owt off sycht :
And thai fled als so hastyly,
That away gat the mast party.
This fycht on Saynctandrcwys day,
Or on [the] evyn, as thai say,
As I devys, here strykyn was.*

Some of the best evidence concerning where the battle actually took place is based on the two roads or ways as they are described. If ever there was a road which goes with the title of this book, then these two are surely old Deeside Ways. Umast is most likely what we would know today as the old drove road from Marchnear to Tullich. There seems no disagreement among the few that have written about the battle on this point. Umast is very much the upper way which, I found, was still in use as a drove road within living memory. Along it incidentally are to be found the Four Lords' Stones. Tohair has been called 'nether' by Simpson, meaning in Scots, lower, however, I think, reading it in context shows it means simply *other* way: the same word is also used in the last verse quoted here and makes complete sense as, other. Quite likely it is the road passing the current Burn o' Vat entrance close to which the memorial stone is placed.

Moat beside the Hall of Logie Ruthven where De Murray's army camped before the Battle of Culblean. Strathbogie and the Atholl men were on the 'Umost Way', an elevated path on Culblean Hill opposite, with Loch Davan between the two opposing camps.

My earlier question regarding the four Lords' Stones may or may not be answered: however, the chronicle in one verse (repeated from above) reads as follows;

*He sayd to **the lordis** in prewate,*
Gyve thai wald trow his cownsalle, he
Suld throw the wode a redy way,
Enwerown quhare thare fays lay

Perhaps more likely the Atholl camp where this was said to have happened;
Hys spere in bathe his handis can ta
And kest it owrthort, and can say,
*" Standis **lordis** a stownd;" and thai,*

The folklore then, that four lords dined on the four stones before a battle suddenly seems more likely. We know the battle of Culblean was fought there or somewhere near and we know now that there were lords present, the chronicle spells it out. This name may be one of the few surviving links apart from the chronicles themselves which may be helpful in placing the other camp or battlesite.

The stones are naturally occurring and located adjacent to the old drove road just approaching the brow of the hill, a logical place to stop. A good place to survey the area is within a short distance of the stones whilst being able to keep just off the skyline.

Melgum Road, Tarland, capital of the Howe of Cromar

There are substantially large boulders in only a few places close to a little path. Have I stumbled onto something through those names? The Clashneach is also located a short distance from the Four Lords' Stones, the first word Clash, being a hollow or cutting, which describes the place perfectly, but what of the second word neach? Neach is likely to be from nich, meaning, horse. Our chronicle tells of De Murray's 800 horse which he left before engaging. Earl

Davy's camp would have had many horses also.

An earlier verse as follows talks of a great stone which is reputed to be the large erratic boulder above the small ford approaching the Vat itself: it may well be but there is also a ford, large boulder and we have the Four Lords' Stones in close proximity by the umast road located above the Vat.

Evyn in the peth wes Erie Dawy,
And till **a gret stane**, *that lay by,*
He sayd, " Be Goddis face, we twa
The flycht on us sail samyn ta."

Nothing here is conclusive, I fear, but I have enjoyed trying to match the chronicle some way to what exists on the ground. Simpson placed the battle site along the umast road near the Marchnear ford; with Earl Davy's camp farther out the old road. Marren in his excellent book Grampian Battlefields suggested the Burn o' Vat and the areas below; the monument put up by The Deeside Field Club is placed across the public road between the two; there is a good case for all and doubtless the fighting was spread over an area. If the chronicle is correct, a ford, a large boulder, a pool, bushes and the umast way are the common factors and that narrows it down nicely to a few spots which some archaeology might one day reveal.

Perhaps the four lords' stones are something more than just four stones and folklore and once more a place name has held meaning down the centuries: we may never know. They have also been called the Mary Stanes or the Four Marys. When we wander along the old drove road we can parallel with history knowing that countless numbers of feet have taken the same old ways and marvel that key historical events took place close by.

As for the Race of Tullich, Grant had this to say.

In February, 1654, was run the much vaunted "Race of Tullich." Glencairn and Kenmure came over from Kildrummy, and endeavoured, but with small success, to raise the Gordons and Farquharsons, some of the Farquharsons had joined, but whether Inverey was one of the number is uncertain. They were encamped on Culblean, some fourteen hundred strong, horse and foot. Colonel Morgan, with six troops of horse and three of Cunnighams's dragoons, advanced rapidly against them. With great cunning he despatched a small party of horse and foot by a circuitous route to gain the high ground on Glencairn's left and rear. This was done successfully;

and the sudden appearance of the foe nearly cutting off their retreat caused such a panic, that it was not a question of fighting hard but of flying fast. The pursuit continued several miles. Over a hundred men were among the slain, and thirty were taken prisoners...

That should perhaps have been the end of this diversion but not all stones were unturned. I was looking at an unusual old ruin near Culblean when a man appeared unexpectedly. We were soon having an interesting conversation about how and why the ruin had such a strange appearance. Bob Esson told me the ruin was called Wester Milton and that the owner had been a painter and decorator who was used to working with cement this explained the leaves elegantly placed on two remaining cement pillars.

It was a lad Sandy Robb that was the last person to have it, around 35 years ago, he kept goats there. He put the pillars onto the place and made the vines around them. A lot o cement work. It was a thaket hoose at one time, then iron on the roof.

Since then we have been over much of the ground together recording folklore. I mentioned the Battle of Culblean. Bob told me that the water clock (a water-powered clock no

Loch Davan left and Loch Kinord from Culblean Hill

BATTLE OF CULBLEAN

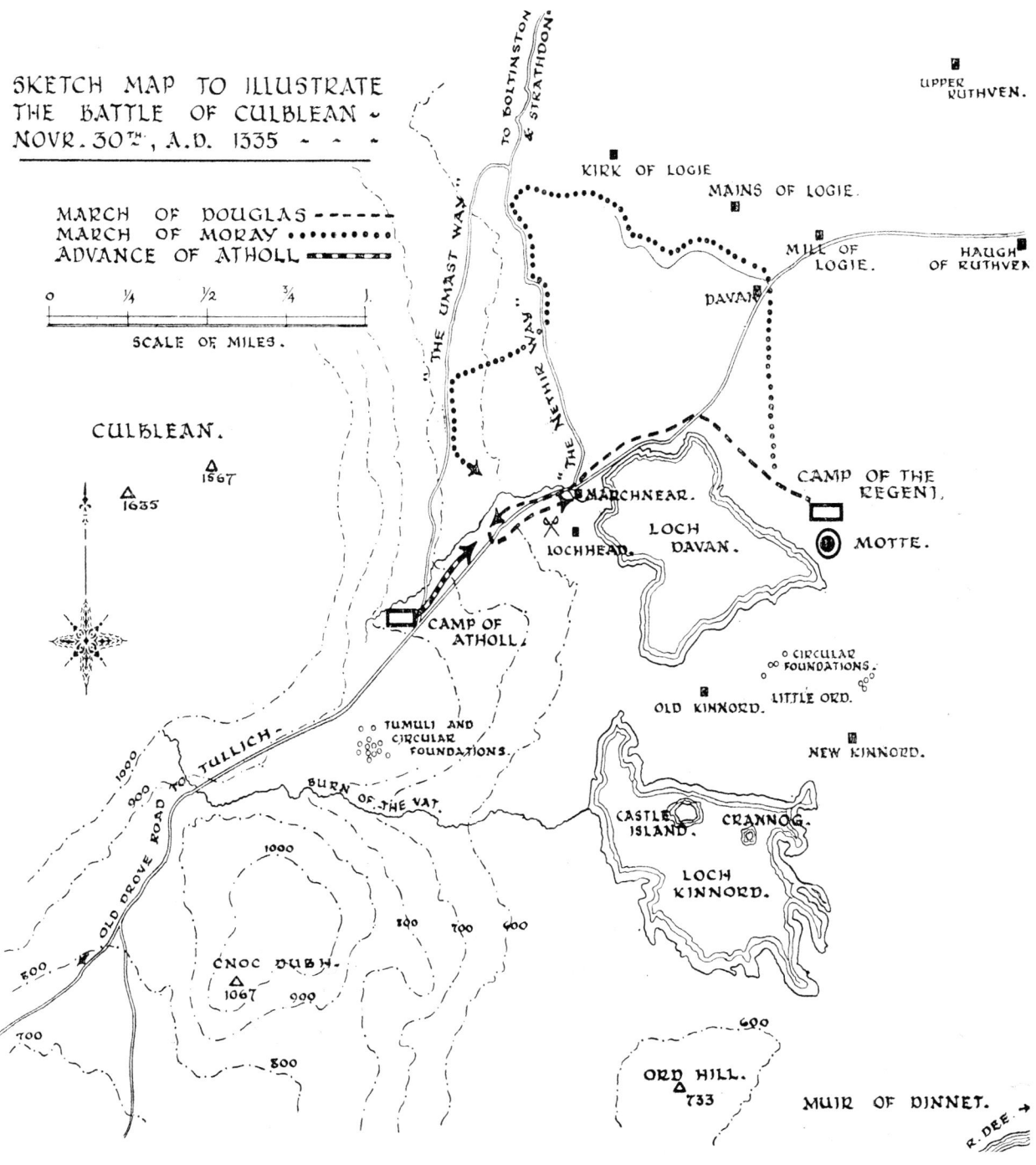

Simpson's interesting sketch map demonstrating his theories published in 1931 by the Deeside Field Club

longer in existence) once held a museum including swords reputed to be from the battle. They were sold on many years ago. I asked Bob if he knew where they had been found, he thought they were up the old drove road (umast road) and then well up the hill. Maybe the site of the battle was not such a mystery after all. *When we were loons we aye went to the Burn o' Vat on a Sunday then down to the Water Clock. The chap there had swords from the battle of Culblean and a gun with a great thick barrel on it. They were found on the road to Marchnear and well up on the face of the hill on the right hand side when heading out to the tearooms. The road goes richt through there.*

I sat at the site of the old moat of Hall of Logie Rothwayne in order to judge distance, it seems that De Murray could probably have seen from there where the Athole men were, directly across from him high on Culblean, he may have seen smoke from their campfires (which still exists in the folklore of the area) and possibly the glow from their fires when darkness fell, giving him a useful guide. Most likely they had been tailed by the Kildrummy party's scouts or indeed the 300 men from Kildrummy who marched into De Murray's camp adding confidence as well as valuable information, being local. They would have had much detail also on the numbers of men they faced and how they were armed with any weaknesses they might have witnessed when under siege. From experience sound travels right across Davan and a conversation can be heard with some clarity from one end of the loch to the other. Looking at the ground, with and without the benefit of modern maps, from the hall we may think him wise to split his party, having decided to go towards the Atholl camp.

Earl Davy might have expected movement at dawn but to be confronted by an army at close distance at first light must have been a surprise but the second part of De Murray's army coming in from the side and possibly from higher up sent panic through the ranks with the

Bob Esson, former gamekeeper at his home

Ruin of Wester Milton with elaborate pillars

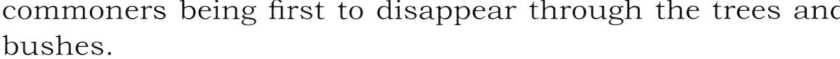

Former resident name in cement at Wester Milton

Remnants of vines in cement at Wester Milton

commoners being first to disappear through the trees and bushes.

I think it's most likely De Murray's party's split either side of Davan. Judging by the ancient settlements between the lochs, he would have had a relatively easy pathway through with the other party heading around the other side of the loch and possibly picking up the umast road. They used the cover of darkness to good effect and given it was in November had plenty of time whichever route they chose. One theory was that they went around by the River Dee. Atholl may have dropped down below the umast road leaving himself more vulnerable to attack from above. It sounds as if De Murray managed to get above them regardless of which direction he came in from, most likely using the umast road.

It has been suggested that this battle took place below the Vat: my only idea in this is that although many of the individual features mentioned by de Wyntoun exist at the Vat such as an oak tree, ford, large stone, there is no mention of the Vat itself. Which you might think would be mentioned in the old chronicles. Although I do wonder about the pool he mentions;

Thiddyr he went, and in a pele
He sawffyt hym and his menyhe welle.

I think its time to leave the subject of the battle and wander along other pathways. The battle though small is regarded as being significant in Scottish History during the wars of independence.

Not so very far away from Culblean Bill and Elizabeth Gillanders told me about the Seely Howe though it was Bob Esson who finally showed me where it is, a large hollow that before becoming forested was a sunny spot and sheltered. An old verse tells of the indignation of its former inhabitants:

Bob Esson shows the author the Seely Howe

Dule, dule to Blellack
And dule to Blelack's heir
For driving us from the Seely Howe
To the cauld Hill of Fare

It seems Blelack laird Charles Gordon called upon the McGregors from Morven when he raised his regiment in the 45 Rising and it is said they had to camp on his estate we might assume at the place called the Seely Howe because this, according to tradition, was why he forced out the fairies onto their new home on the Hill of Fare, fanciful though it is the Seely Howe exists as a place and is in local folklore.

It seems they didn't like their new home on the Caald Hill

The Lump of Culblean where the Deil is said to have ridden through with a pair of horse

Old Oak tree growing from crag upstream from the Vat, close to umast road and ford

of Fare and left a form of premonition or curse. From this we can see the belief in such things still evident in the 1700s and much later. Michie mentions the Lump o' Culblean, a rocky outcrop on the Culblean hill behind which lies a gap that the Deil (Devil) was said to have driven through with a pair of horse.

We might have been forgiven for thinking that when Patrick McGregor was hanged that no one would dare steal cattle. The following entries from Aboyne Estate papers make interesting reading though at a later time.

Huntly & Aboyne Estate Papers. *House of Lords Case. Aboyne v Earl of Aberdeen, 1782*
Tenants right to sheal in Morven
If it attempted to be proved that there is great danger of theft – if sheep or cattle are sent to the forrest without herds.

One of the Cromar people mentions a James Couts in Acha... afterwards in Tarland who was concerned in many thefts in the Forrest & banished for it 20 years ago. To enquire about him, how long ago it was . . . . (before the rebellion).

It was said that 40 head of cattle were stolen from the Bunreach by a Ketteran with whom Couts was connected & that they carried with them to drive the Cattle two boys John McLaggan now in Grodie and James McLaggan in Tullich . . . . .

It seems intended to be proved that some of the Tenants of the ten ploughs of Coul were in use to send their cattle to Morven – to enquire who can dispone this & prove that they had good pasture on the hills to the East & north of them – toward Lumphanan & Lochel.

And to prove that they never shealed in Morven.
Ar. Forbes swears to his losing 2 sheep last year out of 50 – by sending them without a herd.

It is said that sheep are generally left in the forrest till Lambas.

It is said that the Black Park at Wester Morven there was no laboured ground 4 years ago – no marks of Riggs. To enquire how long it has been enclosed & cultivate.

Ar. Forbes says that in summer 1781 at one time 16 of his sheep & at another 20 were poinded by George Reid & Lewis McKenzie & that he was obliged to give bill for 40 pennies each for first fault & for half a mark for 2nd fault.
It is said that the first Settler on Bogganfoul was one Emslie – who was forced to leave Tullich for theft and afterwards to leave Bogganfoul for the same cause.

About 10 years ago Andrew Wall in Davan – Jas. Hendry there & Alexr. Smith in Mains of Logie had a sheal among them – on Tomchirum – James Smith in Leys another.

And that Mrs Cumming in Mill of Dinnet, Robert Cromar & Wm. Ross in Ferrer, John & Peter Machray & Alexr. Mill there had sheals at the same time and place.

Earl of Aboyne's tenants are making improvements upon the part of the hill of Culblain called Bogganfoul – encroachments by Inverey.

Chapter 11 *In the Footsteps of Sandy Davidson*

> *The defender having appeared...and he being judicially interogated by the justices whether he is guilty or not guilty; he declares he is not guilty.*

At a cairn of stones on a hillside in Strathdon, a wild heart beat its last. A free spirit and one of the last free foresters, held in high esteem by many who knew him. I had to find Davidson's Cairn to tie up another loose end from Deeside folklore and as it turned out I was not disappointed. I drove into Glen Buchat and walked out along a track: it was a morning of sleet, cloud and some mist. I had read and heard so much of the man and been inspired by finding a court summons for him, in a box of old papers, that this seemed an obvious place to seek. It was a dour cold November day, but often, if you head on regardless, rewards come, and the mist soon cleared, revealing a wonderful landscape, in the low winter sunlight, of heather moorland, gently rolling hills and stony summits. I did not doubt I would find a cairn, but wondered, if there were several close together, how I would know which was his? Having wandered out the track, I saw a white cairn in the distance: on arriving I felt I was surely on the right spot. I admired its beautiful quartz stones neatly placed: having approached from the moor below the road, I was delighted and surprised to see that his name had been chiselled into the stone, with the dates of his birth and death. That is unusual: there have been many died on the hills down the centuries; more often than not, a pile of stones marks the spot, with the knowledge of whom and when held only within the hearts and minds of those from the glens who found or were connected. If ever there was a place

Alexander Davidson from The Romance of Poaching in the Highlands

for such a man to breathe his last, this was surely it. I felt at peace as I explored the cairn and took my photographs, then went on to explore some large boulders on various tops nearby. I could see why he liked this moorland and found several likely spots where he might have used large boulders for cover when hunting or for shelter. When I was taping the folk of Upper Deeside, he came up in conversation at times but, frustratingly, few remembered their parents or grandparents having much detail for a curious young man trying to see into the past. *One said he could disappear into the waater wi a strae in his moo and they wondered far he had gone till.* Also that: *faan he was found his terrier dog was still on his chest.*

In this case, the records stumbled upon give us possibly the clearest accurate picture of a man I now know definitely existed. Of all the old cairns I have looked at in the past, none matches the simple understated yet appropriate cairn of Davidson. He appears in the literature of a century ago in Michie's Deeside Tales and a sizeable piece is written of him in The Romance of Poaching in the Highlands by W. McCombie Smith. My delay in writing about him was that I could add nothing unpublished about the man, so could not see a valid point. That situation has changed, upon discovering his summons which reads as follows:

Unto the Hon ble His Majesties Trustees of the Peace for the County of Aberdeen. The Petition of John James Roy. Factor for Mrs Farquharson of Invercauld

Herewith,
That Alexander Davidson an alledged Wood Merchant sometime residing in Mar Forest, occasionally in Achendryne and frequently at Durris did upon this eighth day of October last or one or other of the days of said month or of months of September immediately preceeding Hill Game on the Hill Ground belonging Mrs Farquharson of Invercauld in the Parish of Crathie, although not qualified to kill game by having a ploughgate of land in Heritage and not having the permission of the owner of said Lands who is so qualified.

May it therefore please your honours to Fine the said Alexander Davidson in the sum of One Hundred Pounds Scots to the petitioner in terms of the act Sixteen Hundred and twenty one, chap. thirty one, and in the sum of Five Pounds Sterl or other suitable Sum of Expense of Process

Chiselled boulder, Davidson's Cairn; A Davidson 1792 1843 located where he died on the hill of Creagandubh

and to Grant Warrant for levying the same or Imprisoning him till the same be paid in terms of the law.

John J Roy

It seems a remarkable sum of money for the time considering the offence: we can guess that the authorities were out to sort him once and for all.

Alanaquoich 8th November 1831. The Justice having considered this Petition Grant warrant for serving the said Alexander Davidson with a copy of it and of this deliverance and for Citing him to appear personally to answer to it at a court to be held at Ballater upon the fifth day of December next at twelve o'clock noon, and for citing witnesses for both parties for the same time and place.

Chas Cumming JP

The warrant was served by Donald McKenzie, Constable, by delivering to him the written complaint, list of witnesses with a copy of the citation.

...this I did before these witnesses Alexander Davidson in Torgalter (presumably Sandy's father) *and John McHardy in street of Monaltrie.*

It goes on to advise:
The defender having appeared...and he being judicially interogated by the justices whether he is guilty or not guilty; he declares he is not guilty.

James Coutts a gamekeeper residing at Cairnachuine in the Parish of Crathie and the County of Aberdeen, a witness for the Complainer, who being solemly sworn of malice and partial council examined and interrogated; depones that on the Eighth day of October last, he was going on the peat road to the Moss of Monaltrie, and having heard two shots fired, went in the direction in which he heard the shots, and saw a man with a gun and two dogs one of which was a pointer; saw the said man fire a shot caut up with him soon after, and found him to be Alexander Davidson now present as defender; who spoke to the witness and said; I am not trespassing on your Ground: witness enquired, if he was not, what was he firing at, so it looked very suspicious to see a man with a Gun and Dogs on the hill if he was not trespassing: the Defender replied, 'he was going to Gairnside and only wanted to take a shot as it came in course, *and if he had not seen the Witness he might have taken a bird if it came in the way, in conveying the defender of the grounds of Monaltrie, the defender said 'May I take a shot now, witness replied no until you are past Badfantich and out of my sight.*

James Coutts

We might be forgiven then for thinking that this would be the end of Sandy. If he were to be found guilty he would receive this massive fine: if he could not raise the money, then to the jail he would go. But Sandy had pleaded not guilty, hardly surprisingly since his other option led to ruination, or incarceration. From what we know of him, though, it seems he had some strict values: he would observe the Sabbath and not shoot on these days and would not take game out of season. Upon seeing the gentry who at one time employed him, holding shooting competitions on a Sunday day repulsed him and, though he loved to shoot in competition, he would take no part in it. He was

Part of record of events at court in Ballater

fluent in Gaelic and spoke English when not talking the old language of his ancestors.

Witness farther depones that he did not see the Defender kill or pick up any game; that he had a game bag on his back with something in it, but what that was the deponent cannot say; all which he depones to be the truth as he shall answer to God.

Ballater the Fifth day of December Eighteen Hundred and Thirty one; The Justice having considered the above complaint with the proof laid for the complainer, Find the Complaint not proven, will therefore absinifie the defender and dismiss him from the bar.
J Cameron JP

Alexander Davidson's final resting place, a grand spot for a free man of the hills

Chris Cumming JP
Andrew Robertson JP

Quite a lot has been written of Sandy. He purchased standing pines from the Earl of Fife in Glen Derry. This would involve cutting the timber and floating it downstream, which would be no easy task. The old pines were remote and he endeavoured to get them out by floating them to the River Dee and thence to the sawmill he had...*to construct a dam of sufficient size to make a large lake in a long hollow which the ice had scooped out behind them, thus give him water power to float his timber to the Dee.*

The spot is still referred to as the Derry Dam. There was no economical way of floating the timber to market in Aberdeen. In the end he sold back £200.00 of standing timber to the Earl of Fife, who, Michie tells us went under financially without paying Sandy. It was from this point onwards, it seems, he resorted to poaching. He may well have felt justified in his activities, having lost such a substantial sum of money.

I was interested to find the above previously unpublished

instance against the within designed Alexr. Davidson, with a deliverance thereon dated the Eight day of Novr. last; The Defender Having appeared, the said Petition with deliverance thereon being read over to him and he being judicially interrogated by the Justices, whether he is guilty or not Guilty; He declares he is not guilty

Alexr. Davidson
Jas: Cameron J.P.
Cha. Cumming J.P.
Andrew Inglis J.P. &c.

Compeared James Coutts a Gamekeeper residing at Carnachuine in the Parish of Coathie & County of Aberdeen, a witness for the Complainer, who being solemnly sworn, purged of malice and partial counsel, examined and interrogated; depones that on the Eight day of October last, he was going on the peat road to the Moss of Monaltrie, and having heard two Shots fired, went in the direction in which he heard the shots, and saw a man with a Gun and two dogs; one of which was a pointer; saw the said man fire a Shot; came up with him soon after, and found him to be Alexander Davidson now present as defender; who spoke to the witness and said, I am not trespassing on your Ground; Witness enquired, if he was not, what was he firing at, as it looked very suspicious to see a man with a Gun and Dogs in the hill if he was not trespassing; The Defender replied, he was going to Gairnside, and only wanted to take a shot as it came in course, and if he had not seen the Witness he might have taken a bird if it came in the way, in concern the defender of the Grounds of Monaltrie, the Defender said, may I take a Shot now, witness replied, No, unless you are past Badfantich and out of my sight.

+ James Coutts
Ja Cameron J.J.P.

court proceedings match Michie's other anecdote as regards the Invercauld Factor John J. Roy's name. *The big Stane o Cluny* still sits in a pool above the new brig of Dee. This incident happened before the bridge had been built, otherwise the factor could have saved himself a lot of trouble. The stone sits just a few yards upstream from the bridge. Sandy was with the loggers whom Roy was enraged at and their logs were piled in a cairn as they described it on top of the stone. Roy liked the stone because of its shape and usefulness in protecting salmon. Loggers hated it and made a plan to blast the stone. This came to Roy's attention and so he tried to prevent this happening by visiting the stone where the men were working and serving an interdict which it seems was not served in time or ignored. Sandy's men resolved to *slip a log* should the factor come on to the temporary bridge connecting the bank with the log pile. Sandy would have no part in this.

When the factor, attended by a few followers appeared in the distance, Sandy heard one of the men, not one of his company, swear that if the "Tyrant" should come on the bridge he would never go back. He remonstrated against any personal violence being offered to him, however tyrannical he might be, but all to no purpose. Mr Roy, on reaching the bank, determined, against the advice of those who were with him, at once to cross to the cairn. Sandy, observing his intention, bawled out in a voice that rose shrill above the noise of the stream. Don't come, Mr Roy; your life is in danger. "I'll take my chance of that," *replied the courageous factor, and continued to advance...* Sandy repeated his warning and, ignored by the factor, he saw one of the men attempt to slip the log. He leapt on to the log bridge and carried off the factor to the bank just as the way across collapsed whereby he would have been swept to his death. Those who saw the recent spate on the Dee will know the power the water can generate. It seems the opinion at the time was that Sandy had acted very honourably but the factor had been aware for some time of Sandy's poaching exploits and banned him from the estate. Here he was floating timber through the Invercauld section of the river and attempting to blast a noticeable feature. Visiting the scene today in low water, it's easy to think that the stone is so close to one side that he would have been in no danger in any case. However the loggers floated in high water in order to move the logs. Sandy has had much written about him, Michie's account

The big stone of Cluny where the logs piled high and the Factor nearly drowned. A recent high spate has left debris demonstrating the height of water and also why it would have obstructed loggers in the past.

Stone under water viewed from the bridge during August spate of 2014. Picture was taken in the evening after the water had reduced in height. Gauge visible below centre

Old way in Glen Derry among ancient pines.

being the most reliable and original: to this I add the court documents which back up the character of the man. A cairn on a Glen Buchat hill which folklore said existed was surprising in its inscription and construction. Among the folklore and writing, we learn of his handsome appearance, his love of adventure as a whisky smuggler, a log floater and contractor, unafraid of risk and also a poacher of note although not of the worst kind but one with values. He spent nights on the hills and forests and often families would find a hare or bird from the forest hanging in the larder not even knowing he had stayed in their outhouse, by which time he was long gone, pursuing his game across the marches and boundaries of the neighbouring estates. I suspect he was held in high esteem locally partly because of this and that he lived the life he loved in the outdoors free from the control of anyone and unencumbered by material trappings. The wild land provided most of his basic needs.

Chapter 12   *The Last Ritchie o the Torran*   139

The Ritchies gaed intae the Torran in 1816 that's faan they got married the Ritchies were there at that time and could have been for years and years afore that.

I went to see Tom Ritchie the last surviving Ritchie of The Torran, who left when he was called up to the Second World War: his father had given up the farm about the same time. It is typical of the style and type of hill farm from the area supporting a family over decades if not centuries.

The Torran was a small farm on the hillside in Glen Gairn, Upper Deeside. Torran means simply the little hillock. It once supported several families and later the Ritchies.

Tom Ritchie and I went back to The Torran for a walk around. The old farm house had been empty as a home for many years though used occasionally. He told me of an old soldier who used to come and help on the farm especially at busy times. He slept in the barn sometimes working into the winter months. Tom showed me the barn and said he was seldom cold as he bedded down above the horse which he said kept him warm, the heat to rising to where the man slept.

There wis an aald sodjer used tae come and work wi us in the Summer and help wi the hairst he baed in the laaft there abein the horse and sometimes he was here a good while in the winter an aa, cauld ye ken, but he said it wis fine and warm wi the horse in alow him. He wis an aald Scots Guards man and he used tae tell us aa the stories o the Scots Guards and I thocht I'll hae to get intae the Scots Guards and I wis called up and I wis pit intill the Scots Guards. I wis the third Ritchie tae ging, the aaldest brither wis killed at El Alamein the first twa three days.

Willie Ritchie o The Torran before Braemar Gathering 1950.

The Ritchie family of The Torran. Approximately 1878

We walked around to the old horse mill or the mill Laivers as Tom called them. I was pleased to hear an account from him of how he worked the horse mill in the early morning.

I wis the last ane at The Glen Gairn school Willie Findlay gaed tae Crathie and I wis pit oot. There wis folk fae Inverenzie came through the snaa tae the school they hardly missed a day. There's the aald Horse Mill in there I mind on the horse mill, afore ye gaed awa tae school in the mornin ye had tae dae the thrashin. It workit richt up until the aald man gaed oot it wis a good mill ye ken.

There wis twa horses gaed on tae the mill and there were three laivers but we only workit twa it wis aa it nott. They hid a towe fae the bridle tied on till the laivers tae thrash the corn, it wis aye corn we hid, some o them hid barley but it wis aye corn we hid. Ye bruised it for the beasts well ye selt the spare corn or pit corn tae the mill. The mill was used tae thrash the corn aff o the strae. I took the horse roond afore I gaed tae school ye'd tae dae that in the mornin then awa tae school aifter that.

Oh ye nott a horse we hid three a while we kept the foal and we used to play we the foal it wis aafa petted my brither pit me gaed on its back, aye without a haulter ye ken and we hid it inna a cairt and aa that things that wis afore the aald man broke it in.

There wis a bit at the far end faar the gig wis kept.
Mrs Ritchie, who has an interest in family history, continued; *The Fleemans bed in the Shenval and the Leys bed in the Shenval. There wis Leys in the Torran afore the Ritchies gaed in and they wid've been the Leys o the Shenval Tom's great granny John Ritchie married Margaret Leys and there wis Ritchies in there fae that time they widve got intil the Shenval. There wis a lot o different folk in the Torran lang ago. They might have been in the glen longer but they went into The Torran then.*

Tom had some memories of modernising of the road; *It wis afore the war Tom was born 1927 it widve been in the 30's I wis five years aald.*

There is a quarry up the Shenval They metalled the road fae Ballater tae Torbeg oot o that quarry on Cairndoor just

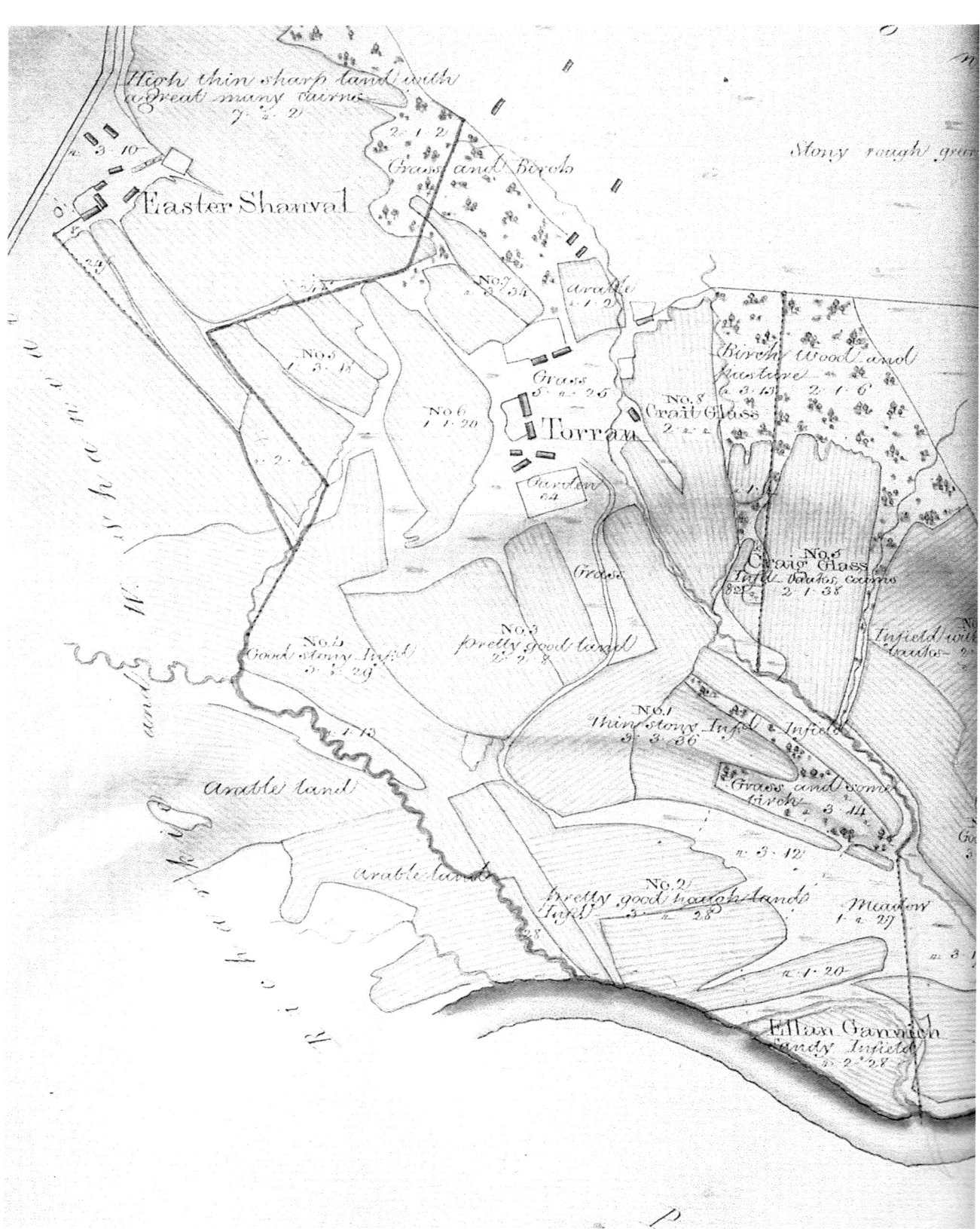

The Torran 1808

afore the war started. They hid a steam engine and the waater for the Torran come fae a well awa fair doon fae it and they hid a pipe fae there tae feed the steam engine and work the crusher. I wis a kid at the school at the time the lads that worked the quarry the lads hid their huts aside the Black Brig up fae Torbeg. This wis metallin the road, afore that it wis large steens wi tar in atween.

Andersons stayed at the Muir Cottage: they aa hid whiskers (beards) apart fae this lad and he wis caad whiskers. Pringles blacksmith finished just afore the war. My father used to go there ai time and then Charlie Clark at the fit o Gairn the next time gae them baith a shot like.

Dalphuil that wis the school my father gid till its the Queens cottage noo a lot o the buildings doon noo but there wis ruins at the side there wis scholars came and bed.

I gaed till the new school me and Willie Findlay wis the last anes the quines gid till the side nearest the kirk and the loons at the ither side.

Willie Ritchie o The Torran
He pit on his kilt and sporran
Though he's growin aald and bald
He'd fecht and die for Invercaald.

We stood inside the old place and admired the old pine linings and fire place. The walls are lined with pine. *I mind faan the waas were lined it was just the bare waas faan I mind on it first.*
We used to lay a bit of the peat onto the top and it burned all night we hid nae sticks to burn they aye had peat and they aye took a bit o turf and that gaed in the back o the fire at nicht and it smouldered awa aa nicht in the mornin ye hid a bit o a fire.

A large metal hook hung from the roof.
We used to hing our ham up there if you wanted bacon you just put yer hand up and cut off a slice we kept a pig, father killed it an aa thing and cut it up and saalted it wi brine in a big dish.

The horse she wis 27 faan she deed, she wis an aald meer we caad her Jeanie.

144   OLD DEESIDE WAYS

Tom Ritchie at the door of The Torran with horse. Note the cheese in the cheese press. 'The horse She wis 27 faan she deed she wis an aald meer ue caad her Jeanie'.

THE LAST RITCHIE O THE TORRAN

Tom Ritchie revisits The Torran 2011.

We had a walk over the ground the Ritchies had worked for so long.

That bank there that's the Lang Ley, it gings richt ben to the road. There's nae whin busses noo it's strange how things disappear and other things come up. We caad the burn the Richarkarie burn and that ither ane is the Tamnavey burn

There was tragedy too at The Torran. It was the 6th January 1902. The burn had swollen through melting snow. Insignificant and harmless normally, the burn was now in spate. Unfortunately the planks that normally would have been sufficient for crossing were precarious.

That's the burn my auntie wis drooned in. She wis up at the school; the bakers I think she wis up aat and he wis taakin up her shoes they were doon at the shoe maker and she gaed doon tae collect them and she slippet on the plank she wis supposed to hae half a croon change fae her shoes and she still had it in her haan faan they picket her up. Aye it's a tragedy it wis a spate. It wis the 6th January 1902 faan she wis drooned.

Much later on Fermin up there wis gaen oot the last year my faither worket there he said he lost £100.00 that would be thousands noo. He had tae give the place up a year afore that wis just afore the beginning o the war then the farms couldna ging wrang.

The Ritchies never had a tractor at The Torran apparently, just the four-legged variety, Tom used to joke.

One day during the early days of motoring a car became stuck on the Shenval Brae, still a difficult place in winter. The occupants were extremely cold and probably suffering from the onset of hypothermia. Tom and his father spotted them luckily and went to their aid and finally pulled the car out of the drift with the horse. They took the occupants across into the farmhouse and heated them and gave them soup and tea. For many years after at Christmas time a hamper would arrive from Faulkner and Mason London as a thank you.

We left The Torran, sitting silently where it always has against the lower slopes of Cairndoor, another name seldom used today. The main road across to Donside neatly cuts across the hill adjacent to The Shenval. The old walls had witnessed the laughter of children playing and the lives of many unfolding to the steady change of the seasons over many decades. The future of these old places is uncertain. Some have been done up to become larger homes, one or two are still farmed commercially and some fall into ruin and eventually stones are removed for other purposes. Whatever the future, the past has revealed something of the old ways at The Torran and places round about. This one in particular had one family occupy it for a very long time.

There was one question I had tucked away for a couple of decades, it concerned the last wolf.

Chapter 12   **The Last Wolf**   147

What darkens the door? It's a long time since the cry of a wolf was heard in the glens of an evening: the haunting howl echoing around the great corries and glens would have been unmistakable. The relationship between man and wolf was always likely to be strained, especially in the days when a family's survival depended entirely on a few animals and a scratched existence on marginal ground in a remote area. The wolf long ago lived and hunted freely in the corries and wild parts. The last wolves in Scotland were hunted to extinction in the mid 1700s. When researching for *In the Shadow of Lochnagar* I found that the last wolf killed in Glen Gairn and possibly anywhere in this country came up in conversation as follows;

It wis the old folk in Gairnshiel that told me aboot it. It was some time in the 1700s some laddie had been oot in the hill and raised it in that den and he ran home and told his father. They waited till the next day and they gid up and killed it in the Den.

Artist impression of Wolves in Scotland painting by Martin Ridley

Alex Duguid, a former resident of the Gairn, told me exactly where this occurred: the narrow gully sits up on the hill above the former farm of The Shenval. I have been there many times, it's become a favourite spot when heading out or returning from the hill. I have seen beautiful snow cornices form there in winter. An old lichen covered cairn above the gully may well have been erected at the time. Anything of significance often warranted a cairn and one was erected to the last wolf killed in Glen Muick, though, unfortunately, it seems, it was removed during road alterations. The old residents would have known that was a rare occurrence and decided, some time later, I suspect, that these were the very last wolves in these glens. The whole point of putting pen to paper was to preserve the old folklore and place names of the past and so I became aware that there were a few important anecdotes concerning one of our last wild predators that deserved preservation.

The Shenval in Glen Gairn the last haunt of the wolf. Road filled in with snow

At the time of our chat a couple of decades ago as I write, Alex suggested I contact the Ritchies who, he thought, could be the only family who, due to their deep roots in the glen, might know the exact year it was killed. The last wolf I have seen written about was killed in Invernes-shire in 1743 but the Gairnside folk claimed their wolf was later than this. It was a couple of decades before I met Tom Ritchie, who at the time of writing, is in his eighties: their family association in the glen stretches back through time. After a long chat and a subsequent visit to his old home in the glen: I recalled Alex's suggestion and asked Tom if he had heard anything of wolves in the glen: almost

Hand written document concerning the last wolf in Glen Muick

to my surprise and delight, Tom told me the following.

Well, my father hid a story aboot this lad who wis inside the wolves' Den, this lad wis inna the hole for the young anes or something like that and there wis ane o the lads ootside. The wolf come in aboot and the lad ootside grabbit its tail as he gaed inna the hole and the lad inside the hole shouted, he shouted: its hell of a dark, fits adee? (whats darkening the door?) *Ane o the lads wis oot and he grabbit the tail as the wolf gaed in. He said: if I let go this tail ye'll seen see fit wye it's so dark and he telt us faa the lads were and aa, but I canna mind faa it wis. That's aa I heard, the aald man* (his father) *telt us that!*

I was pleased when a few months later, I found the following paper in amongst some old notes; *The Last Wolf in Glenmuick:*

Last wolf was killed in Glen Muick between the Linn and the Loch. A cairn was raised to mark the spot. A man who had some sort of a gun got safely past the place where the wolf was known to be, and he met another going in that direction & gave him the gun. This man shot the wolf.

A Scottish wolf born here but in captivity at Kincraig Wildlife Park. Species European or grey wolf coincidentaly located not very far from where the last wolves were killled

One of the men was going South over the Capel and met the other coming North – The first man said he saw a wolf as he came and seeing the other had no gun he offered in case

Jock Harper at Aal - Mhad Barn or wolf rock most likely a former wolf den

he might need it.

There were Wolf McAndrews... Wolf McKenzies, Wolf McGregors, descendants of children who had been taken away and brought up by the beasts. "Whats dark'nin the door? If the tail breaks ... whats darknin the door" This is of a man who went to get back a child & the she wolf returned.

I had already been shown Wolf Corner years ago in Glen Muick by John Robertson. It fits the description above as it is just west of Allt an Sneachda, burn of the snow. I could scarcely believe the similarity. I had thought maybe that would be the only surviving part to the story until the above came to light.

As for the idea of bairns being taken away by wolves, of

course that would have done little to improve the wolves' survival in a country which also had a popular folktale like Little Red Riding Hood.

Grant, in his *Legends of the Braes o' Mar,* had something to say on the last wolf which has some similarity to above: the location is more or less the same as the Glen Gairn folk had said:

The last wolf seen in the country was killed near the Shenval of Gairn. He was seen prowling about by the people of Richarkry. The old farmer there asked one of his sons to try him with his bow, for old age had marred his own strength and skill. The youth wished for nothing better. He bent the bow, quickly took aim, and let the arrow fly. The wolf seemed to keep its course untouched, but the hill was so steep, that the arrow could not have failed to come in contact with the earth. Immediate search was made, and it was found. When the old man saw it he wept for joy that he had a son able to draw his own bow, and send an arrow to such a distance. On examining it, he cried out excitedly :

"Run, Run ; it has gone clean through." They had not to run far, for there surely lay the wolf dead before it had reached the neighbouring burn.

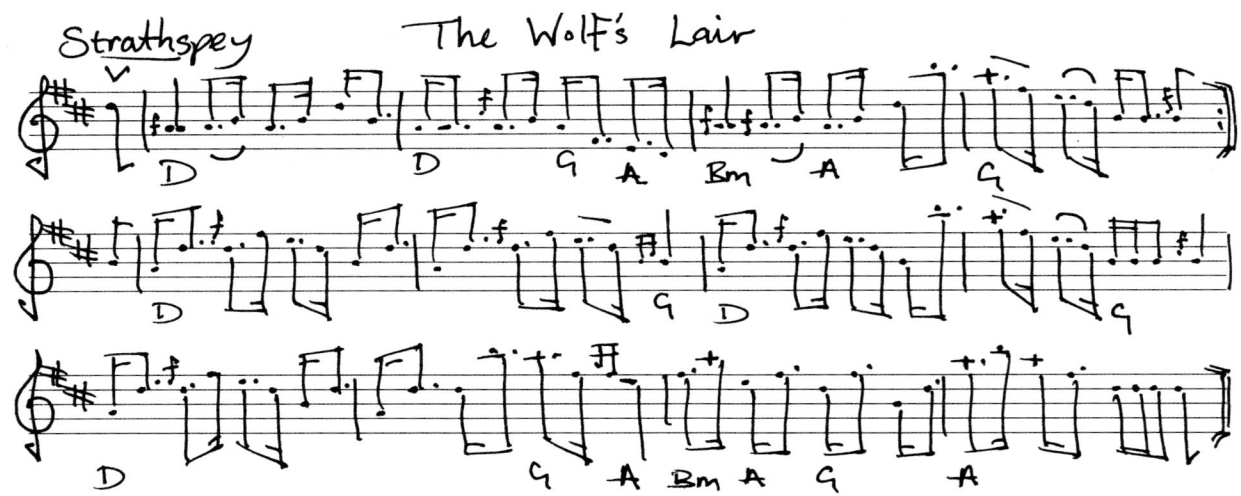

Grant also tells us of a McDonald infant who was taken by a wild boar or wolf and was deposited with its young. It's a pretty fanciful story but he was said to have grown up with the wolves, then been captured by the neighbours of the farm from where he had originated. He eventually was tamed and settled with a daughter of the house. His mother, it is said, recognised him from a mark on his face. Grant goes on to state that the pair produced a wild but brave race.

Both Glen Muic and Glen Cluny claim the legend, with this difference:- Glen Muic, true to its name, attributes the taking away of a child to a wild-boar, and furthermore bestows on that child the name of Andrew, deriving from him the McAndrews in the three united parishes; Glen Cluny stands by the wolf, and holds that the McDonalds, long called "Sliochd a' Mhadaidh-Alluidh," of whom there are yet three families in Braemar...One at Altchlar, one at Ardearg, Corriemulzie,

Wolf Corner, Glen Muick

and the third in Glen Cluny itself – are the descendants of this hero.

I have seen documentaries on certain families where hair grows thickly all over their faces. It may be that this is the source of the belief in folk descended from the wolf.

Beyond Glen Muick to the south is Wolf Hill, a flat-topped grassy hill with remains of stone structures reputed to be areas where animals could be taken in at night for protection against the wolf. There is also Wolf Grain, which is a small branch of a burn to be found North East of Mount Keen. Close to The Shenval in Glen Gairn, up the junction between Glen More and Glen Beg, Bill Gillanders told me of a place which Jimmy Ross, the old keeper at Candacraig, had told him about. It was lined with stones and known as The Wolf Pit. It's pretty likely that was a hiding place used for trapping or hunting the wolf, similar to the Boars' holes which we discovered and I have written about before and it was described as such. Interestingly, this is reasonably close in proximity to the location where the last wolf in the country was said to have been killed near The Shenval. The

Glen Gairn from above Shenval

Inside the wolf den Aal - Mhad Barn.

John Robertson at Wolf Corner in Glen Muick where the last wolf in that glen was killed

Gaelic for wolf is Madadh-allaidh: recently it came to light that there is a place on Craig Nordie phonetically quoted by longtime resident as Aal-Mhad Barns or Mady Barns. This is a hollow below a large boulder which Jock Harper told us his father used to walk up to on a Sunday afternoon and have a sleep. What we have here most likely is a former wolf den with the pronunciation being very close to the Madadh. According to Adam Watson, who pointed this out to me and studied the Aberdeenshire Gaelic dialect, the last syllable is often left off giving the pronunciation Aal Mad Barns.

Away out the Dee towards Glen Geusachan we have old settlements called Allt Clais Mhadaidh which translates as, burn of the hollow or cutting of the dog or wolf.

Satisfied I have put to paper some of the anecdotes of the wolf in these parts, the readers can mull over the possibilities for themselves and debate whether a child could survive in a wolf pack. What is beyond any doubt in my mind is that the wolves were here and close to habitation at times. This partly explains the need for stone holding pens out in the remote areas and also that the localities of the last of these animals was where they have said they were. As for hearing a wolf cry in the glen, it howled its last in the mid 1700s, never to be heard again though, coincidentally even today we would not have to travel too far to see one, though admittedly in captivity. I told Paul Anderson of the place as we walked out one Sunday morning to enjoy the low hills. He was captivated by the theory of the wolf lair and the stories I had uncovered. Within days he had composed two pieces of music which are included here for others to enjoy. His mastery of the fiddle can evoke and enhance a place.

Standing in wild Alaska at the end of the unmade road I heard the wolves howl in the wilderness and mountains somewhere in the forest just above. It doesn't then take too much imagination to think what that would have sounded like here back in the 1700s and beyond. Through the local folk with long lineages, place names and exploring these places I found there was just surviving folklore of the very last wolves in Scotland.

Final Thoughts

The old ship Invercauld would be heard from few lips today yet it was a significant loss at that time imagine floating timber from the forest to Aberdeen turning it into a ship and sailing across the world only to be shipwrecked so far from home. Some names have endured like Sandy Davidson, one of the last free foresters living life on his own terms. Baron Ban Farquharson: what an interesting life he led, escaping death on Culloden moor: then being reprieved on his day of execution, then returning to Deeside to build bridges, repair roads and have the vision to see a town develop on the moor. The Rev. George Brown described him in a word as being possessed. I think its more likely he had found a real purpose. The last wolves left a legacy on which I have just managed to pick up only through many years of taping folklore. As for Ian Grant, I became interested many years ago when I was told of his whisky-making antics, through meeting his relatives and old friends I see a much clearer picture not just of one man but life in the upper reaches of the River Dee. Also, I was pleased to see through the eyes of a guest at one of the grand old shooting lodges back in the 1800s. As for Culblean, that battle is such a long time ago it is a wonder that we have a record such as De Wynton's Chronical, though some questions remain for me: that's healthy. All this, especially the folk I have met and got to know well, have made me appreciate even more living on Upper Deeside. I hope this will be a continuing journey in years to come exploring the *Old Deeside Ways*.

We didn't have sweets and things when I was young, said Grandfather Joe Murray, *instead, we would chase the bumble bees. We would follow a bee across fields until it went into a hole in the moss, then we would scrape into the place where it had disappeared with our fingers and dig out these individual small sacks of honey, we would suck out the sweet honey often with our hands covered in earth. We called the bumble bees the Mossie Bummers because they aye nested in a moss bank. That was the best we could do for sweets chasing the bumble bees across, fields and bogs and fences: it was great fun, we would run for miles.*

Acknowledgments

I would like to thank Dr Seumas Grant for writing the foreword to this book, Sincere thanks to all those listed below whose company, I have enjoyed in the course of writing this book and for the anecdotes, information and photographs that have shaped it.

Special thanks to

Mr A Alexander, Ballater
Mr A Anderson Newburgh
Mr P Anderson, Tarland
Mr R Bain, Crathie
BLHG, Ballater
Mr & Mrs I Brown, Braemar
The Dartmoor Trust
Mr J Dorward
Mr H Butterworth, Ballater
Mr A Downie, Ballater
The late Mr W Downie, Ballater
The late Mr A Duguid, Ballater
Mr R Esson, Grodie
Captain A C Farquharson, Invercauld
Mr L Fraser, Blairgowrie
Mr G Forbes, Aboyne
Mrs E Gillanders, Dinnet
Mr R Gillanders, Edinburgh
The late Mr W Gillanders, Dinnet
Mr J Harper, Crathie
The late Mr D McDonald, Ballater
The late Ms N MacDonald, Braemar

The late Mr C McIntosh, Braemar
Mr & Mrs H Mackay
Mr R Mitchell, Braemar
Mr & Mrs D Murray, Ballater
Mr & Mrs J Murray, Ballater
Mr B Murray, Ballater
The late Mr L Murray, Ballater
Mr G Muir, Banchory
Mr Ian Norrie, Coupar Angus
The late Mr T Ritchie, Lumphanan
Mrs L Ritchie, Lumphanan
Mr J Robertson, Crathie
Mr R Robertson, Ballater
Mr N Shepherd, Aberdeen
Mr G Smith, Ballater
Mr H Stewart, Ballater
Mr I Taylor, Aberdeen
The late Mr J Taylor, Ballater
Dr A Watson, Crathes
Mr C Wright, Braemar
Mr A Yule, Ballater

References and Bibliography

In the Shadow of Lochnagar, Ian Murray. 1992

The Dee from the Far Cairngorms, Ian Murray. 2000

The Cairngorms and Their Folk, Ian Murray. 2010

Place name discoveries 2015, Adam Watson and Ian Murray

The Place Names of Upper Deeside, Adam Watson and Elizabeth Allan 1984

Taped interviews by Adam Watson with Donald McDonald (DM) and Ian Grant (IG)

All other interviews carried out by Ian Murray

Deeside Tales, John Michie 1908

Legends of the Braes o' Mar, John Grant 1876

The Campaign and Battle of Culblean, The Deeside Field, W. Douglas Simpson 1931

Andrew of Wyntoun's Orygnale Chronicle 1420

The Prehistoric Antiquities of the Howe of Cromar Alexander Ogston 1931

The Kelpie, poem by Violet Jacob

Grampian Battlefields, Peter Marren 1990

Previously unpublished papers of William Brown, Crathie

From diary papers, My first day in Mar Forest by Horatio S.J.Ross Esq

The Coming of the Camerons 1944 Director Frank M Marshall

All recent photographs published here were taken by the author. Most historical pictures have been collected over 25 years and were given to the author by the informants with permission to use them. In some cases it is now impossible to tell who the original photographer was. The author has tried to credit all involved and hopes to be forgiven any omissions or inadvertent copyright infringement.
The author of this work accepts no liability for damage to property or personal injury resulting from anything described within this book. At all times the walker is advised to give due regard to sporting and landowners' rights. The description of any place within this book does not imply that a right of way exists.